GOD SAID "I Promise"

A refreshing way
to look at the
Ten Commandments

Debbonnaire Kovacs

Pacific Press® Publishing Association
Nampa, Idaho
Oshawa, Ontario, Canada

All Bible references are taken from the New American Standard Bible except where otherwise indicated.

NASB. From the New American Standard Bible, copyright © by the Lockman Foundation 1960, 1968, 1975, 1977. Used by permission.

Edited by Jerry D. Thomas
Designed by Tim Larson
Cover illustration by Justinen Creative Group ©

Copyright © 2000 by
Pacific Press® Publishing Association
Printed in the United States of America

ISBN 0-8163-1779-8

00 01 02 03 04 • 5 4 3 2 1

CONTENTS

Dedication
To Elder Ed Motscheidler,
who assured me I could.

CHAPTER ONE

A Threat or a Promise?

"THOU SHALT NOT!"

Given the present state of human nature, those words seem almost calculated to bring out the worst in us. Or, as Paul put it, "the Law came in that the transgression might increase" (Romans 5:20). It is easy to understand why so many have an idea of a vengeful, angry God, thundering forth judgments. The problem is, those with that mistaken idea did not read the rest of the verse—in either case! They didn't notice "I AM the Lord your God, who has already rescued you." They didn't see "but where sin increased, grace abounded all the more."

Even when we know and love God, we tend to think of His laws as negative, difficult concepts. We try so hard to obey, and we fail so dismally. It's even worse if we have confused law keeping with salvation, and think we must obey to make God love us, or to gain His approval, or to make ourselves fit for heaven. Nothing could be further from the truth. In fact, nothing is more likely to make a person give up on heaven altogether! Why, then, did God word the commandments the way He did?

When God descended to Mt. Sinai to talk to His long estranged, now reunited children, He had to give His law in a simple, distilled form. Anyone who works with children knows it is much simpler to tell them the few things they must not do than to tell them the thousands of things they are welcome to do. But I don't believe He ever intended for us to get the idea that His law is therefore a negative thing. If it is a transcript of His character, then it certainly includes infinitely more than those ten imperatives.

Jesus made that clear when He gave His commentary on the law during the Sermon on the Mount. He told His listeners that they not only had to keep from killing someone, they had to keep from hating, keep from insulting, worst of all, actually love their enemies! They had to come to the place where they were willing to be like Him—to sacrifice themselves for those who did not even appreciate it.

And there is still so much more to learn that we will be studying the law of God for all eternity. Yet on the other hand, all that infinite complexity, distilled at Sinai into ten commands, can also be simplified still further—into just three short words.

God is love.

If we are to get away from worrying hopelessly about those "Thou Shalt Nots," it will be necessary to change our thinking. First, let's accept once and for all that God really is love. That means He's not a negative, mean, judgmental Being.

Many people stop right there. "God is love. So He must not have written those negative, impossible commandments. It was Moses. And he got them from the Code of Hammurabi . . ."

But let's go a little further. Let's agree that God wrote the commandments, did so with His own finger, in fact. We'll assume He didn't write them in English (King James or any other vintage), but we'll also assume He's been overseeing their multiple translations all these centuries. So let's take a look at the language.

We can start with the word "shalt," or its modern form, "shall." Though out of fashion in the United States today, "shall" is actually the first person future form of "will," as in "I (or we) shall go to the store." When used with second person—"you shall"—it correctly means a promise. "Yes, you shall go to the fair."

Interestingly enough, some of the best examples of this are found in nursery rhymes, many of them current when the King James and other older English Bibles were printed. Remember this one?

> "What! Lost your mittens?
> You naughty kittens!
> Now you shall have no pie!"

> "Found your mittens?
> You good little kittens!
> Now you shall have some pie!"

Here's an even better one for our purposes:

> "Pretty maid, pretty maid, wilt thou be mine?[Will you choose to be?]
> Thou shalt not wash dishes, nor yet feed the swine, [clearly a promise]
> But sit on a pillow and sew a fine seam,
> And feast upon strawberries, peaches, and cream!"

What a revolution in thinking it would cause if we thought of the commandments that way! Take, for instance, "You shall not steal." Suppose a person had a serious problem with stealing. Suppose he thought God could not love him because he could not stop stealing. Then suppose he learned about the free gift of salvation. To his grateful astonishment, he learns that God loves him now—while he is still a thief!

Does God say to him sternly, "You shall not (read 'must not') steal," or does He assure him, "You shall not steal—I promise!"

Imagine the difference to this struggler's future. He wants to stop stealing. It is the greatest desire of his life. Nothing could comfort him more than the certain knowledge that God has the power to change him, for good!

What if Jesus' words, "If you love me, you will keep my commandments" (John14:15), weren't a threat, or a challenge, or even a measuring stick, but a simple promise? He said Himself that all the law and the Prophets hung on love for God and love for others. What if He really meant it? What if all we have to do is love Him and love Him and love Him, and He will do all the transforming?

Then the law, which was a measuring stick of death before our conversion, will become a shining goal—something God holds up to us and says, "This is how I am, and this is how you shall be when I am through with you. You shall not lie or cheat or steal anymore. You'll enjoy a holy Sabbath, and love your family, and be content with what you have. You'll be called by My Name, and it will mean something."

By now you may be protesting, "Come on, Debbonnaire! You're surely not going to try to teach theology through nursery rhymes!" Don't worry. It's not necessary. All we have to do is look at the Bible, starting right there in Exodus 20.

We cannot possibly understand the rest of the law of God unless we clearly understand the first sentence of it. "I am the Lord your God, who brought you out of the land of Egypt, out of the house of slavery" (Exodus 20:2). Notice the past tense—"brought." God delivered the Israelites before they began to keep the law. He delivered them before they had even heard the law.

Their ancestors had known it, of course, but after generations in Egypt, most of the people had practically forgotten the existence of the one true God. In Egypt, the people worshipped the sun, jackals, frogs—even insects. You'll notice that almost every one of the ten plagues involved one of the false gods of Egypt and decisively showed God's power and the helpless silliness of the entire Egyptian religious system.

Now that God had their attention, He was about to begin teaching them how salvation really worked so that they in turn could teach the rest of the world. For the next several centuries, God tried to convince His people that His promised salvation came through a heart relationship, like the one their father Abraham had shared with his Lord. Moses told them (and told them, and told them . . .),

> "You will [or thou shalt] seek the Lord your God, and you will find Him if you search for Him with all your heart and all your soul . . . Know therefore today, and take it to your heart, that the Lord, He is God in heaven above and on the earth below; there is no other . . . And you shall love the Lord your God with all your heart and with all your soul and with all your might . . . I have set before you life and death . . . so choose life in order that you may live, you and your descendants, by loving the Lord your God, by obeying His voice, and by holding fast to him; for this is your life and the length of your days" (Deuteronomy 4:29, 39; 6:5; 30:19-20).

David, too, taught his people that God looked on their hearts, and that salvation came from His love, not from their worthiness. In fact, his Psalms are filled from beginning to end with insights into the love and all-sufficiency of God, and with promises of complete salvation: "Salvation belongs to the Lord: Thy blessing be upon Thy people" (Psalm 3:8). "For the Lord takes pleasure in His people: He will beautify the afflicted ones with salvation" (Psalm 149:4).

David's last counsel to his son Solomon was, "As for you, my son Solomon, know the God of your father, and serve Him with a whole heart and a willing mind" (1 Chronicles 28:9). Then David prayed, "O Lord, . . .give to my son Solomon a perfect heart to keep Thy commandments" (1 Chronicles 29:18, 19). Obviously David had learned that the heart came first, and that a heart that could obey was a gift from God.

David's prayer was answered, for his son's first request from God, when he was a young king, was that God would give him an understanding heart, to discern good and evil (See 1 Kings 3:9,10). Solomon, like all of us, had to learn some things the hard way, but in the end he, too, taught the people, "Wait for the Lord, and He will save you . . . Victory belongs to the Lord" (Proverbs 20:22; 21:31).

Then came a whole string of mostly ungodly kings, so God raised up prophets to tell His children of Israel the truth about salvation. The prophet Isaiah taught and wrote:

> "Then you will say on that day. 'Behold, God is my salvation, I will trust and not be afraid;' . . . Therefore you will joyously draw water from the springs of salvation" (12:2, 3).

> " 'My righteousness is near, My salvation has gone forth, . . . My salvation shall be forever, and My righteousness shall not wane'. . ." (51:5, 6).

> "I will rejoice greatly in the Lord, my soul will exult in my God; for He has clothed me with garments of salvation, He has wrapped me with a robe of righteousness" (61:10).

Jeremiah, the "weeping prophet," kept pleading on God's behalf, " 'Return, O faithless sons, I will heal your faithlessness.' . . . Surely, in the Lord our God is the salvation of Israel" (Jeremiah 3:22, 23). Still the people refused to listen. They wanted to worship anything they wanted to, in any way they desired. So God left them to Nebuchadnezzar who would teach them a lesson they would never forget.

In the aftermath of that great destruction, through his tears and in spite of the apparent hopelessness, Jeremiah insisted, "The Lord is good to those who wait for Him, to the person who seeks Him. It is good that he waits silently for the salvation of the Lord" (Lamentations 3:25).

After the Babylonian captivity, the Israelites never looked at another idol, but they still did not seem to catch on to worshipping God from the heart. Now they thought doing all the right things would save them. At the very end of the Old Testament, God was still begging, "Return to Me, and I will return to you . . . For you who fear My name, the sun of righteousness will rise with healing in its wings; and you will go forth and skip about like calves from the stall" (Malachi 3:7; 4:2).

Then God sent His own Son. By that time, Israel had built up a whole new religion of their own, a religion of not just ten, but hundreds of "Thou Shalt Nots." And if that teacher Jesus wouldn't endorse all their "Thou Shalt Nots," then He couldn't possibly be the Author of the original ten. So they resolutely shut their hearts against Him.

After three and a half years of walking from one end of the country to the other, touching, loving, healing, pleading, "I AM the Way, the Truth, and the Life . . . Come to Me . . ." Jesus stood on the hill overlooking Jerusalem and sobbed. "O Jerusalem, Jerusalem, who kills the prophets and stones those who are sent to her! How often I wanted to gather your children together, the way a hen gathers her chicks under her wings, and you were unwilling. Behold, your house is being left to you desolate!" (Matthew 23:37, 38). Soon He stretched out His arms and died for them anyway. He couldn't help it. He loved them. He loves you. He loves me.

So now, it is finished. God has provided for the rescue of every man, woman, and child on this planet. Each one must decide whether to accept rescue or stay with the ruler of this present darkness. To accept rescue, all we have to do is say, "Yes! Come into me! Save me!" Then "you who believe in the name of the Son of God . . . may know that you have eternal life" (1 John 5:13).

After, and only after that transaction is complete, the new child of God has a chance of beginning to make an effort at commencing to try to learn to keep His law.

To that end, the goal of this book is to try to look at the law in a whole new way. We will try to get at what Jesus meant we should do when He listed the things we were not to do. And we'll find the possibilities are endless. We'll find that, more than we ever thought possible, love really will fulfill the whole law—every jot and tittle.

How?

I strongly encourage you to have a Bible at hand as you read this book. It is more than anything else a study book, and there will often be times when reference is made to a certain text or passage, and you will need to read them to understand what follows.

At the end of each chapter, there will be a HOW? section. It's all very well (and all too easy) to read a book, even the Bible itself, and say, "How interesting! How inspirational! I ought to do that!" Only, that tends to be the end of it.

We don't want to make that mistake. We want to learn how God wishes us to view His commandments, and how He wishes to make them real in our lives. Our salvation is complete, praise God, but the Bible says there's more after that, if we want it.

In 1 Corinthians 3:9-15, Paul says some strange things.

> You are . . . God's building. According to the grace of God which was given to me, as a wise master builder I laid a foundation, and another is building upon it. But let each man be careful how he builds upon it. For no man can lay a foundation other than the one which is laid, which is Jesus Christ. Now if any man builds upon the foundation with gold, silver, precious stones, wood, hay, straw, each man's work will become evident; for the day will show it, because it is *to be* revealed with fire; and the fire itself will test the quality of each man's work. If any man's work which he has built upon it remains, he shall receive a reward. If any man's work is burned up, he shall suffer loss; but he himself shall be saved, yet so as through fire.

I don't claim to fully understand this passage, but some things seem clear. The foundation is Jesus, and His life and death for us. Now obviously, if we reject and tear down the foundation itself, we will be lost. As long as we don't do that, but found our lives firmly on Jesus, we are saved.

But a foundation is not a whole and complete building. We can build different things upon that foundation. We can, without rejecting Jesus and His salvation, do some pretty foolish things with our lives. I know—I've done it.

12

And I know what the fire feels like. I'd much rather build something lovely—something made of the gold of God's commandments (Psalms 19:7-11;119:72, 127), the silver of wisdom and instruction (Proverbs 2:4; 8:10), and the precious jewels of a gentle and quiet spirit (1 Peter 3:4). Wouldn't you?

In the HOW? section, we will explore how to make the "gold of obedience" real and lasting in our lives.

CHAPTER TWO

I AM, Therefore You Shall Be

I AM Yahweh your God,
who delivered you from Satan's ground,
and rescued you from sin, slavery, and shame.
Let Me be first and last to you.
Let Me live in the center of every moment of your life.

Have you ever tried rewording the Ten Commandments using positive language? When it says "Don't do this," what does it mean to do? Why not try it, before you read any further? Warning—you may discover complexities you had not imagined. But you'll also find the commandments take on a richness that fits your own life in a very personal way.

If you have never tried rewording texts in your own language, here are some ideas that may get you started. First, ask the Holy Spirit to guide you. He's the only One who knows just what you need to learn today. Then read the text in several different versions of the Bible, if you can. You can even use the lexicon in the back of a good concordance to find out what the original Hebrew or Greek words are, and what they mean. They often have more layers of meaning than the English words into which they have been translated.

You don't have to know anything about Greek or Hebrew to use the lexicon. Opposite the word you look up in the concordance will be a number. Look up that number in the lexicon, and there you have it. You're a language scholar, and you didn't even know it.

Next, look at the text phrase-by-phrase and reword the phrase in a way that has special meaning for you. In my example for the first phrase of Exodus 20:2, I have given "Yahweh," the personal name of the Eternal, self-existing God and otherwise left the phrase as is.

The next phrase is, "Who brought you out of the land of Egypt." What does it mean to me? God never brought me out of Egypt. In typical Hebrew fashion, the second half of the sentence repeats and defines the first half. "Out of the house of slavery (or bondage)." That's what Egypt means in this context. I have never been a slave in Egypt, but I have certainly been a prisoner on Satan's ground.

I have served time in a grim prison indeed—the Shadow Land they call clinical depression. It wasn't 400 years, but it seemed like it.

How can I describe it? Life—simple, ordinary, daily life—becomes impossible. Brushing your teeth—let alone feeding your children—is an enormous accomplishment. Emotions are by turns totally silent and numb, and terrifyingly magnified, like the distorted monsters of nightmares. A tiny little annoyance, or sorrow, or even joy can tip the balance into what feels dreadfully near to insanity.

If you've been there, you know. If you haven't, I hope you never do know. Here is a sentence from my journal from those days: "I lie immobile beneath a mountain of pain, sorrow, and responsibilities so huge that if I lift just one finger to attempt to meet one of those responsibilities, or shift one of those cares, the whole thing will fall and crush me instantly." But then again, here's another: "I can no longer hold on to You, Lord. So You'll have to hold on to me."

And I knew He would. I knew, thanks to the teaching of a godly mother before I could even talk, that Jesus would *always* be with me, no matter what. I couldn't see Him, hear Him, or feel Him. I was often very angry at Him. But I knew He was there. Like the Israelites, I wept,

"How long, Lord?" Where was Moses? Where were the miracles? Why didn't He deliver me?

What I didn't understand was that although God's Emancipation Proclamation is sometimes dramatic (and sometimes not), it's only after that that the years, even centuries, of in-depth, desperately difficult spiritual therapy and rehabilitation begins. It seems like centuries to me, anyway! At least it does now that I know what normal feels like.

I also know, looking back, that a lot of the sins that I so berated myself for in those days were both bred by that depression and fed it. Everything from laziness and bad temper because I felt so powerless, to the pride of refusing to find help because God and I were going to handle it on our own. I thought the depression itself was a sin. I *ought* to be able to feel better and to behave like a Christian woman no matter how I felt! It was a cruel and pointless spiral.

But God was always there and always working. Even then, on my better days, I accepted and believed that God *had delivered* me, whether it felt like it or not, and that if I died (which I sometimes would have welcomed), I would see His face when I opened my eyes. He had "delivered me from Satan's ground, and rescued me from sin, slavery, and shame."

Which brings us to the heart of the first commandment. "You shall have no other gods before Me." Why would I want to? What is God really asking *you*? What is it He wants you to do? Ask Him, and then write it your way.

Done? Good. Now read the commandment as you've reworded it. Once the Holy Spirit has helped you to personalize it, the same old text sounds like a whole new concept, doesn't it? Jesus said this was the most important commandment. Of course, He chose to quote the wording in Deuteronomy 6:5: "You shall love the Lord your God with all your heart and with all your soul and with all your might." It's the same commandment, and we can never hope to understand the other nine until we understand this one. God put it first for a reason.

The Ten Commandments—Ten Promises—begin with an introduction—a salutation. If I am going to read a set of instructions, I want to know they were written by someone who knew the subject. I don't think an owner's manual for a pickup would be very useful if it was written by someone who designed and built refrigerators. So God begins by saying, "This is who I am. Not only am I the One who created all life, but I just finished rescuing you from something you could never have gotten out of by yourself. I love you." (See Exod. 20:2; Deut. 5:6.)

If we think for a moment about what the Israelites had just gone through, we can see that they had every reason to believe that God knew what He was talking about, and that He had the power to back up any promises or commands He made. Even more importantly, they knew they mattered to God. They didn't know it because someone told them so, or because they read it in a book. They knew it because they had watched Him save them from a hopeless situation. From several hopeless situations! They were free, and they were on their way to the Promised Land. They were ready and eager to hear anything God had to say. I can relate to that! Can you?

Suppose God had come to the Nile instead of Sinai, and laid out the Ten Commandments before He rescued the Israelites? Suppose He had said, "I'll rescue you if you obey Me first." Many people seem to think God's law operates that way. But that isn't how He does things. First He saves us. Then He asks something of us: He asks us to love Him first, last, and best.

I have had friends who were struggling with the idea of Christianity say to me, "This God of the Bible is so proud and arrogant! All He says is 'Praise Me, love Me, put Me first, worship Me!'" And they were very serious. It really seemed that way to them.

Well, of course, if God really exists, if He is really omniscient, omnipresent, omnipotent, eternal, and all that other stuff, then He has every right to be as arrogant and proud as He wants. But there's only one problem with that. Well, two.

One is, when Jesus was on earth, He was nothing like that. The other is, the Bible tells us to be meek and humble. Yet we are supposed to be like God. How, then, are we to reconcile these two seemingly opposing ideas? Well, here's a news flash for Planet Earth. (The other worlds already know this.) God already *is* the alpha and omega, the be-all and end-all of all that ever has existed or ever will exist. He is a God of incredible powers I cannot even begin to imagine, who could end everything with one word. He is a God of three personalities—a thing I can no more comprehend than I could comprehend a four-dimensional cube. He is a Being so far above us and our thoughts that even to call Him any particular gender would be impossibly presumptuous if He hadn't started it first.

The very idea that this God could so humble Himself as to allow puny, rebellious natives of a minor planet to decide whether to *permit* Him to be God in their lives is shocking! Is it possible that to God, this world and its inhabitants are so treasured that He doesn't even like to see words like "puny" and "rebellious" used about them? Is it conceivable that He would love us so much that He would risk His own Son's life to rescue us from a pit of our own making?

Is that His voice I hear? It is not demanding, but pleading, "Please let Me love you. Please come to Me and walk with Me, and let Me do for you all the amazing, unthinkable things I do for My children on unfallen worlds.

"Please?"

How?

What does it mean to let God live in the center of every moment of our lives? What is at the center of this moment, right now? Is it this book, my ideas about God, your ideas about my ideas . . . or is it God? Do you love Him? Does He matter more than anything else in life?

All you have to do is cherish that love, nourish it, choose to spend time with Him. There are two important ways to spend time with God. One is specific time, and that is the most important and should come first. Yes, first—before you brush your teeth, before you eat breakfast, before you get the kids up. First.

Don't misunderstand me. I don't mean you must put your formal Bible study time first. Some people's brains are lively at dawn and some aren't, and the lively ones sometimes seem more than a little insufferable to those of us who aren't! What I mean is that the heart of your devotional life—that is, the act of greeting God and devoting yourself and your day to Him—must come first. You can choose your own time for heavy-duty study and prayer, according to the personality God gave you.

Ask yourself:

> How can I center the first waking time of each day around my Lord?

> What can I study in the Bible that will help me to love God better?

> What shall I pray about?

Don't forget, you are not through praying until you wait and give God a chance to answer you. Stay quiet and leave your heart open to Him. You may or may not "hear" anything in your heart, but you can be sure He will be loving you more than you can imagine. You may like to keep a prayer journal about what you say to God, and what He says to you.

Now you're ready for the day, and for the other way of spending time with God—general time. Your mind will be on many different things during the course of a day, and that's the way it should be. God has given you responsibilities and gifts and trials, and He has no desire for you to become a hermit and neglect all those things.

What He wants is for you to be aware of His presence with you, in the way a toddler playing near his mother's feet is aware of her and her love. If he has a question, if something frightens him, if he makes something he's proud of, he turns to her without even thinking of it. It's automatic. (Yes, I said mother, and that's what I meant. See if you can find all the times in the Bible that God uses maternal imagery rather than paternal to describe His relationship with you.)

Ask yourself:

How can I let God live His life in the center of:
my family?

my work?

the big crisis I'm facing?
_____?

At the end of the day, spend another specific time with God.
Ask yourself:

What can I thank Him for?

What do I need forgiveness for?

What shall I pray for?

Then remember to listen. And lie down in peace and sleep. For if God is in the center of your heart, you can be assured you are safe in the center of His.

CHAPTER THREE

I Shall Be Your God

When I AM the center of your life,
you shall look upon the heavens, filled with starlight or sunshine,
the earth, clothed in brilliance and teeming with life,
the oceans, cradling continents with their power,
and you shall see My face and feel the touch of My hand.
You shall not be confused into venerating the object,
rather than its Maker.
You shall pass on to your children the assurance of my love and mercy,
rather than the hatred and fear
that leads to sin in all its self-perpetuating misery.
I AM all to you—I want you all to Myself.

In a way, you could say that the first commandment is the only one we're supposed to obey. Every effort of our lives as Christians should be directed toward building a beautiful relationship with God—letting Him be the first, last, and center of every moment. The rest of the commandments are all instructions about that same thing—how to put God first. They're also promises, straight from the mouth of God Himself, about what your life will be like as you learn to put Him first.

The second commandment often seems so old-fashioned, at least to those of us in the so-modern western hemisphere. Who makes idols anymore? When preaching about this commandment, pastors say things like, "Of course, you probably don't have a golden image in your home. But you can make idols of TV, clothes, sports heroes . . ." And that is certainly true. An idol is anything at all, including good things like church and even the Bible, which we allow to mean more to us than God does. But this promise is really about worship. And the issues are as timely as tonight's news.

The first phrase is interesting. "You shall not make for yourself . . ." It is impossible to make for yourself a God. Either there is a God or there is not, but you can't make one. If there is no God, it is pointless to pretend there is, and to make something, set it up, and pray to it. On the other hand, if there is a real God, who could have the nerve to create a make-believe one?

If God is to be first in our lives, He must be the only One we worship. This is so important that He took great pains to be all-inclusive in His list of that which we must not worship. "Or any likeness of what is in heaven above or on the earth beneath or in the water under the earth." That pretty well covers it, wouldn't you say? God made all these things, and He intended that we should see Him in them. So it is true, in one sense, to say that God is in everything. Even that great intellectual, Paul, said people could get enough evidence from nature alone to know the truth about God, and therefore there is no excuse for anybody to say they don't know anything about Him. (See Romans 1:20, 21.)

Unfortunately, there have always been people who take that idea too far, and say God is a life force that is in everything, and that is all He—or It—is. You might say this is a very old idea whose time has come. It's one of the most popular theories on the planet today. And this makes no sense. If there is no God, where did humans get the idea that there ought to be one? And if there is a God, how did He get reduced to this force thing?

We don't have to look very far for the answer. This is one of that old liar's best lies. You see, to make up a really good lie, you have to have a lot of truth in it. Satan either knows that, or else he's just not creative enough to make anything up on his own, because every single one of his lies has truth somewhere in it, and the best ones have a lot of truth in them. That's why this particular lie is so prevalent today. After all, we are educated and scientific and sophisticated, now. Nobody could catch us with that old idea of spirits in trees and rocks these days, could they?

Certainly not—unless he mixed in a lot of other good stuff like unity with each other and the world, a sense of deep contentment with ourselves and our place in the scheme of things, wise stewardship of this planet, and insight into the harmony and rhythm of the cosmos. All of which God invented, not Satan!

It is crucial to understand this—all of these things draw the human soul because God intended them to. That's the way He made us. And so we find ourselves once again, in an age of incredibly expanding knowledge, living in a world in which pantheism is a daily reality. Satan, in his demonic cleverness, has set up a whole system of "reality" that includes all of the factors that God built into life when He created this perfect world. He includes unity, happiness, freedom from crime and disease, power and wisdom, even eternal life and gives it a thrilling name—the New Age. How exciting! How alluring!

There's just one thing missing. It's a sort of major thing. Well, actually, it's the only thing. The thing without which there is literally nothing but death. It's God.

Jesus warned us that the Last Great Deception would be so overpowering that it would deceive, if possible, even saved believers (see Matthew 24:24). There is in fact only one way to escape it. We must learn to let God be first, last, and everything to us. If we choose Him, He has promised that we shall not worship or serve those idols or ideas, and that He can even break the cycle of misery that our parents and grandparents may have been perpetuating.

While we're at it, let's take a good look at that strange phrase, "visiting the iniquity of the fathers on the children, on the third and fourth generations of those who hate me." Is this a threat? Is God saying, "You'd better be good, or else! If you're bad, I'm going to be so mad, I'll punish your children and their children!"

The Jews and other societies of the time did, in fact, tend to think this way. In Ezekiel 18, God declares very plainly what He thinks of such a point of view. Read the whole chapter. Notice especially verse 20: "The son will not bear the punishment for the father's iniquity, nor will the father bear the punishment for the son's iniquity." Jesus said it again when He was here and His disciples asked who had sinned and caused a man to be born blind. (See John 9.)

Well, then, what does this mean? Is it still a promise? I suppose the correct term for a negative promise would be "warning."

Consider this paraphrase: "The choices you make will tend to be self-perpetuating in the lives of your offspring. If you refuse to follow Me, if you set up false gods of one kind or another and won't let Me live My life in you, how will your children know any differently? Even if they choose to follow Me, their lives will be plagued with the results of your bad choices."

I knew a young man I'll call Adam. He used to be chilled with terror as he came home from school each day. What would Daddy do today? Would he beat Adam? Or Mama? Or one of the others? Worse yet, would it be one of the days he wanted to "play"? For a long time nobody knew, not even the church where the family never missed a Sabbath, what hell life was at home. But eventually Adam's daddy went to prison for a long, long time.

How does a boy learn to be a daddy? The way God created him to—by watching. When Adam had children, babies he loved desperately and worked so hard to support, he was determined to be different. But life was hard. He'd married young (to escape), and sometimes had to work two or even three jobs. As the stress mounted, to his horror, Adam heard ugly words coming out of his mouth, and saw even uglier actions taking over his hands. It was as if he had no control. Adam hated himself with a passionate hatred. How could a holy God feel any differently about him?

"Please, please," God is saying in this passage, "think about your choices. They will not only affect you, but all those around you!"

Scary, isn't it? But don't worry; the sentence doesn't end here. "But showing lovingkindness to thousands, to those who love Me and keep My commandments." Other Bible versions say "showing mercy." Why? Because Jesus knows where Adam came from, and He can trace cause and effect.

Over the years, Adam has learned about forgiveness, mercy, and how God can change a life. Adam could tell you that Jesus has all the mercy He needs to carry you through if you are also suffering from the choices of those who went before you. If you stick with Him, He really is "able to keep you from stumbling and to make you stand in the presence of His glory blameless with great joy" (Jude 24). As blameless as if you'd never done it! What an awesome promise! More than that, your godly choices now will give new hope to your children and grandchildren. So how can we make this seemingly impossible blessing a reality in our own lives?

Listed in this second promise, there are four specific, positive actions that will put God in His place on the throne of our lives: Worship Him, serve Him, love Him, and keep His commandments. Let's look at each one.

1. Worship Him.

What does it mean to worship God? My dictionary calls worship "reverence or devotion for a deity; religious homage or veneration . . . intense love or admiration . . . to adore." I think worship might be the automatic response to seeing God as He really is. When we really see His power and righteousness, we are overcome by a kind of fearful awe and humility. When we really see His incredible love and patience, we feel joy and adoration. And when we know—really know—this great God has accepted us in spite of our sinfulness and that He treasures us just for ourselves, all these feelings overflow in incredulous praise.

Praise is the heart of worship. Praise means giving God the credit for everything good in our lives. It is the expression of our growing love for Him. And it happens both deliberately, in the specific time we spend with God, and automatically, during our general sense of His presence all day. When a word or action of ours causes someone else to see a bit of God's love and glory, we have praised Him.

2. Serve Him.

As the current of love between us and God grows deeper and wider, we find ourselves wanting to do something for Him. If we ask Him, and wait for His guidance, He will give us jobs, little and big, to do with Him. We will wait on Him, not as a servant, but as one set free, and the results will astound us. We will keep turning back to God in even more praise—or for more patience, when results are not what we expected. We find serving Him is not at all drudgery, as we feared it would be. It's fun!

3. Love Him.

That's easy—now! It may not have been at first. We may have been frightened of God, or worried about what He would ask of us. Or we may have been afraid He wasn't really there at all. It's impossible to prove God to others, but that doesn't mean it's impossible to know He exists. When we meet Him, we know it! And when we find out how much He loves us, we can't help loving Him back.

4. Keep His commandments.

Uh-oh! There's that "Thou shalt not" thing again! Don't worry. We've come to it in the right order this time. Now that we know how to worship and serve and love God, now that we know for ourselves how impossibly much He loves us, we don't get confused about a perfectly simple word—"keep." What does "keep" mean? No need to get out the dictionary this time. We learned this before we learned to say "yes." Keep means it's yours. It means you get to take it home and nobody can take it away from you. Keep means put it in your treasure box and show it off on special occasions. Keep means, if it's kept long enough, it becomes part of you and you couldn't give it up if you tried.

Remember that major premise-minor premise business you hated in high school? Well, let's figure this out, now.

Major premise: The commandments are the transcript of God's character.

Minor premise: The second commandment promises that we shall keep the commandments. (Right so far?)

Conclusion: The character of God is ours to keep.

Incredible, isn't it? Peter says it even more clearly. "He has granted to us His precious and magnificent promises, in order that by them you might become partakers of the divine nature" (2 Peter 1:4). Partakers of the divine nature! And all because we decided to let God be first, last, and everything in our hearts.

How?

Let's look in more detail at the four actions this commandment promises us.

Ask yourself:

Since God is first, last, and everything to me, how can I . . .

. . . worship and praise Him in a way that will show Him how I really feel about Him?

Try this. Read the last few Psalms. Then write one of your own and sing it to your Lord in secret. Did you know He'll sing back? Read Zephaniah 3:14-20, and especially notice verse 17. You won't believe your eyes!

. . . serve Him in a way that will show others how spectacular He is?

Personal ministry comes under this heading. Do you know to what personal ministry God is calling you? He has one for everybody. If you don't know what yours is, ask Him, and then talk to your pastor or a trusted friend. Read and learn about spiritual gifts and ask the Holy

Spirit to show you yours. When you find your ministry, you'll know, because no work will have ever made you so happy.

. . . show my love for Him in a specific way today?

. . . learn to keep and treasure His commandments, instead of thinking of them with guilt and fear?

CHAPTER FOUR

The Name of Names

When I AM the center of your life,
I shall write My own Name upon you
and wrap around you the mantle of its protection.
You shall cherish that Name and bear it with honor,
never treating it lightly,
but understanding fully its meaning and power.

What *is* in a name? To our pragmatic society, a name seems to be only a label, used for the convenience of identifying something. But historically names have been much more than mere tags, and even today, as detached and impersonal as we often are, there is evidence of the deep meaning names can hold.

In many primitive societies, one person had many names. (Speaking of labels, what does the word "primitive" mean? Most people think it means backward, coarse, even stupid. If you look it up, you'll find it means prime, or first. Sometimes it even has overtones of "causative." We can learn a lot from primitive societies.) A new baby was given a name at birth, usually by a parent. This name might memorialize some event around the birth, or it might refer to a personal characteristic of the baby's looks or personality. It might even be something the mother saw while in labor, and took as a sign.

Later, the adolescent earned or was given another name, perhaps by the elders of the village or tribe. Again, this name had some meaning to the group. It could be something the child was, or something the family hoped he or she would become. In adulthood, particularly if the person accomplished something deemed important by the group, yet another name could be chosen or bestowed, honoring that achievement. This was often the name in which a person took the most pride because it symbolized the person he or she had become, and showed an important contribution to the group.

Another way to change one's name was by taking someone else's name. Historically, there have been three main reasons why a person might bear another's name: as a slave, as an adopted child, or because of marriage. Slave names could be defined as naming turned inside out. A slave name is a name that you do not earn and do not want, a name that bears no resemblance to you or to your real, God-given life. A slave name may be the final insult heaped upon a life already torn apart.

In the case of adoptions and marriages, changing last names today seems to be mostly a matter of habit, convenience, and easy record keeping. But we are reaching a time in our society when names are once again being seen as something more than labels. In recent years, some who felt there were overtones of slavery or possession in carrying the name of a father or husband have chosen names of their own instead. Sometimes those who do this follow the older customs of choosing a name in honor of a characteristic or accomplishment.

Sometimes a name change, rather than representing a new stage of development or growth in life, represented an entire change in direction. Someone who had been a warrior and decided to be a peacemaker changed his name accordingly, and so on.

In some societies, people had secret names, shared only with a chosen few. Their families might know, or only their best friends, or spouses. Or the name might only be known to the person and their gods. Names like this were not just labels. They bore the essence of one's personhood—they were "who you really were." Many believed that a person could gain great power over another, if he could only find out that secret name.

Well, if history interests you as it does me, you may find all of this fascinating. If not, by now you are wondering, "Why is she leading us down this primrose path, and what's it got to do with the third commandment?"

Just this: when God spoke the third commandment, that word "name" meant more to His listeners than it may to us. All of the above principles of naming were present in the societies of biblical times, and most of them are illustrated in the Bible. Rebekah named her first son Esau because he was red and hairy, (Genesis 25:25), but she named her second Supplanter (Deceiver) because he grabbed his brother by the heel.

Poor Jacob lived up to his name for many years, even though he promised to follow God, and tried to do so. Then one memorable night, the supplanter had it out with God Himself. That was the turning point, as it always is. After God trounced him soundly (and easily) He said, "From now on, you won't be called Supplanter, but He Who Strives With God, because you have fought with God and won" (Genesis 32:28).

What? *Who* won? Remember, we're not in the real world, we're only in the mirror world. Everything is backwards here, and it's only when you lose that you win. Jacob—I mean Israel—was starting to figure that out.

Israel named the place The Face of God, and never forgot it.

There are many stories like that in the Bible. In those days they named not only people but everything else, and all the names had real meanings. When the meaning was no longer appropriate, they changed the name. Saul and Paul were probably just Greek and Hebrew forms of the same name, but according to my lexicon, the name Saul is related to the word that means "asked" or "inquired", and Paul is related to the word that means "cease", "desist", and "quit". That seems pretty appropriate. Sometimes God has to hit us over the head with a lightning bolt to get us to cease and desist, and realize that He is the answer to all our questions.

I could go on and on with names from the Bible, but if you find them interesting, you'll look them up yourself. There's just one more principle we ought to note, and that is not the taking of a name, but doing something "in the name of" someone else. We have the idea today that saying "in Jesus' name, Amen" is the full sum of what Jesus meant when He said we could ask things in His name.

But in His day, and for many centuries before and after He lived here, great houses had stewards who had almost complete control of their masters' estates and fortunes. The steward could hire and fire, buy supplies, make decisions regarding farms and businesses and investments, all in the name of his employer. A steward's power was limited only by his relationship with his employer. If they knew each other well, and the owner found the steward trustworthy and responsible, the day-to-day running of the estate could be left almost entirely in the steward's hands. On the other hand, the steward always kept in mind that he was making decisions regarding another's property, not his own. He made the decisions he believed his master would make, not necessarily those he would make himself, and if he wasn't sure, he asked.

If a steward had little contact with his employer, he could make all the wrong decisions, and when the day of reckoning came (literally the day the accounts were reckoned up and reported), he would lose his job.

I recently heard a story about a man whose credit card company called him and asked, "Are you aware that over $5,000 has been charged to your credit card in the last few days, from Hawaii?" The man was shocked. He had just gotten married, and was on his honeymoon in Hawaii. But the card wasn't lost. It was his new wife who had done the charging. I've often wondered what happened in that marriage. It was enough to make him wonder just why she had taken his name, don't you think?

I myself remarried just a few years ago, and am very aware that when I do business I am depending on my husband's years of excellent credit. I would never want to do anything to mess that up, and am, in fact, working to build my own good credit history, too.

Would you like to have a rubber stamp of the signature of a millionaire? You could—if the millionaire knew and loved you, and could trust you to do with his possessions just what he would do himself. That is what "in the name of" means.

When we understand thoroughly what the ancients thought of names in general, we gain a much richer vision of the biblical concept of the Name—or rather the Names—of God. There are dozens, maybe hundreds of names for God, each with its own specific meaning, and all of them wonderful. All of us have heard of the One Name, usually rendered Yahweh or Jehovah, which the Hebrew scribes held so holy that they would not say or write it, for fear of inadvertently profaning it. In our growing and very precious familiarity with our Father and Friend, have we lost too much of that sense of reverent awe at the omnipotence, omniscience, and omnipresence of the great I AM?

Throughout the Bible, from Genesis 4:26 to Revelation 19:13, the name of God holds within it the power and personality of the Godhead. When Moses asked, "Whom shall I say sent me?" God answered, "I AM WHO I AM . . . thus shall you say to the sons of Israel, 'I AM has sent me to you . . . The Lord, the God of your fathers, the God of Abraham, the God of Isaac, and the God of Jacob, has sent me to you.' This is My name forever, and this is My memorial-name to all generations" (Exodus 3:14, 15).

During the deliverance from Egypt the name of God was the symbol of power and might, and later the laws of Moses were filled with injunctions not to profane or blaspheme the holy name, and promises of blessing that would come through that name. (See especially Numbers 6:23-27 and Deuteronomy 18:14-22.)

During the rest of the Old Testament, prophets such as Isaiah and kings such as Hezekiah pled for God's help when the people were in trouble. Since everyone knew the Israelites were God's special people, called by His name, they pled for His help on the premise that it was His name that was on the line.

In the Psalms, the word "name," specifically of God, is mentioned 93 times. Here are a few especially compelling examples.

"May the name of the God of Jacob set you securely on high!" (20:1).

"Save me, O God, by Thy name, and vindicate me by Thy power" (54:1).

"The Lord is great in Zion, and He is exalted above all the peoples. Let them praise Thy great and awesome name; Holy is He" (99:2).

Jesus, the First and Last Word on God, enlarged and deepened our knowledge and understanding of His name. In His model prayer He instructed us to hallow God's name, later He promised to be with those who gathered in His name, and in John 13 through 17 He expanded the glory and power of God's name beyond our imaginings.

He also warned against taking God's name in vain.

"Many will come in My name, saying, 'I am the Christ,' and will mislead many" (Matthew 24:5).

"Not every one who says to Me, 'Lord, Lord' will enter the kingdom of heaven; but he who does the will of My Father who is in heaven. Many will say to Me on that day, 'Lord, Lord, did we not prophesy in Your name, and in Your name cast out demons, and in Your name perform many miracles?' And then I will declare to them, 'I never knew you; depart from Me, you who practice lawlessness' " (Matthew 7:21-23).

Perhaps this is a good place to think about false name-calling. This text is saying that calling Jesus "Lord" does not make it true unless you really accept Him into your life as Lord. A reverse of the same principle is true, at least on this sinful planet. The fact that someone calls you something does not make it true. The only thing that can make it true is your acceptance of it.

That is why it is so important not to attach labels, especially hurtful ones, to children or others whose boundaries are not strong. That old saying, "Sticks and stones may break my bones, but words will never hurt me," is not a statement of truth, but a decision. It is a choice that can be made only by a strong person. If you choose to "take the name of God," then His naming of you as His child supercedes all other names from all other sources.

So the name of God is synonymous with power and love. What, then, does it mean to take His name? We don't need to make a difficult theological concept of it. It simply means to tell Him we want to belong to Him—to be adopted by Him—to be married to Him. When you told Jesus you didn't like your life anymore, and you wanted Him to live His life in you instead, you took His name. You are called a Christian now.

What people see when they see you determines in part what they will think of God. Does that scare you? Good! Because the more it scares you, the closer you'll hide under His wing; and the closer you hide under His wing, the less you'll remember to worry about what others see in you; and the less you worry about you, the more you'll think about Him and about them, and the more they'll see Him in you. Did you follow that? Never mind. Just remember the sticking to Him part.

The Bible closes with a curious thing about names. Watch this progression:

> "I know you hold fast My name" (Revelation 2:13).

> "To him who overcomes . . . I will give him a white stone, and a new name written on the stone which no one knows but he who receives it" (2:17).

> "He who overcomes shall thus be clothed in white garments; and I will not erase his name from the book of life, and I will confess his name before My Father" (3:5).

"I know you . . . have not denied My name" (3:8).

"He who overcomes, . . . I will write upon him the name
of My God, and the name of the city of My God, . . . and My
new name" (3:12).

There follows a lot about a dragon and a beast and their name, and
those who receive this name, and what happens to them. Then we see
the Lamb and the 144,000, with "His name and the name of His Father
written on their foreheads" (14:1).

Next the Lamb becomes a fearsome warrior. "And His eyes are a
flame of fire, and upon His head are many diadems; and He has a name
written upon Him which no one knows except Himself. And He is clothed
with a robe dipped in blood; and His name is called The Word of God"
(19:12, 13).

Then the grand finale—"And there shall no longer be any curse;
and the throne of God and of the Lamb shall be in it [the New Jerusa-
lem], and His bond-servants shall serve Him; and they shall see His
face, and His name shall be on their foreheads" (22:4).

The name of God means power, all the power of the universe,
available to you on request for His business.

The name of God means protection from the powers and principalities of darkness that are more afraid of you than you are of them,
when you bear that name.

The name of God means love, more than you dreamed possible.
You'll feel His overwhelming love within, and find you're able to love
others you never thought you could love.

The name of God means joy forevermore. Don't take it in vain—
take it for all it's worth!

How?

Make a study of all the names of God you can find, and decide
which ones mean the most to you, and why?

List all the names by which you might be called.

How do each of these names influence your behavior?

Which name(s) is/are the most important to you, and why?

Using a concordance or one or more of the verses in this chapter, find a promise that is meaningful to you, in which God promises to give you His name. Memorize that promise and meditate on it with God.

CHAPTER FIVE

God's Signet Ring

When I AM the center of your life,
you shall go about your daily work with a heart that is always at rest.
I have set aside and blessed the seventh day of each week
as a special day when you and I shall celebrate that rest together.
As the anniversary of My creation of the world,
and of My recreation of you,
the Sabbath is the signet ring of My power and dominion.
That holy celebration day shall hover on the edge of your mind
in remembrance and anticipation.

The older I grow, the more grateful I am for the blessing of having known the Sabbath from my earliest days of life. In my family—before we knew how to count off the days of the week—we started asking on Tuesday, "Is it Sabbath yet, Mommy? Is it, huh?"

There is something in the very atmosphere on that day that seems to set it apart from all others. I wonder sometimes why everyone doesn't notice it. There is a shimmer in the air, a softness in the sky no matter what the weather, a clarity of birdsong, and a mantle of contentment wrapped around the heart. The Sabbath is one of the greatest gifts of our Father, one of only a few things still left to us from our lost Eden.

This commandment is already a promise, already written in positive language, and yet what a negative people have managed to make of it over the millennia! For most of history, the Sabbath has either been ignored completely, or made into an intolerable burden. Isn't it strange that the only commandment that begins with the word "remember" is also the only one that is now largely forgotten, even by Christians? Oh, we go to church, most of us, but do we really celebrate a Sabbath?

Let's pretend that we have never heard of a Sabbath day, and look at just what the Bible alone says about it. Ask God to cleanse your mind of all preconceived notions, even those you are sure of. Maybe especially those you are sure of! It is a very worthwhile study to take an exhaustive concordance and look up every mention of "sabbath," "sabbaths," and "seventh day" and study them all with prayer. Obviously we do not have the space to do that here, but we will skim over the entire Bible for the main teachings about this day of days.

The story of the Sabbath begins with the story of this world. Genesis 1 tells the story of Creation, and ends it in Genesis 2:2, 3 with,

> And by the seventh day God completed His work which He had done; and He rested on the seventh day from all His work which He had done. Then God blessed the seventh day and sanctified it, because in it He rested from all His work which God had created and made.

So God made the first Memorial Day. Remember, He didn't create this world for sin. When He first set the Sabbath aside and made it holy, it was intended as a Memorial Day, an anniversary, which He would share with His new children forever. Adam and Eve's first complete day of life was spent with their Father in the Garden, celebrating a joyous new life. I imagine angels gathered there to celebrate the Grand Opening of the new world, too. Who knows—maybe even people from other worlds came! What do you suppose they did that day?

Then came sin, and the ruination of all God's plans. No, not all His plans. He had planned for this eventuality too. From the shambles of Edenic bliss, God salvaged three gifts for His brokenhearted children—Sabbath, marriage and the family, and work. And He promised another—the greatest gift of all, a gift which would fulfill all other gifts—the gift of His Son.

Now Sabbath became something different. Now it was a Memorial Day in the sense of our Memorial Days, a day to remember and honor something lost, and to vow anew never to let the lost die in our hearts. Now Sabbath was a looking back, probably a very painful memory for Adam and Eve, and a looking forward with hope and courage to the day of restoration. Most of all, it became a keepsake, a day to make as much like Eden as possible. It became a day to remember that though sin had done its deadly work of separation, still God was with them—with us—anyway. It became a promise.

What happened to the Sabbath in the antediluvian days? My guess is that it would have been the first thing lost, because only then could humans, created in the image of God, become so evil that all they thought about was how to imagine and accomplish more evil. (See Genesis 6:5.) Only the few heard the whisper in their hearts "Remember!" So few! And they kept (that is, held on to, treasured) the Sabbath, their link to the Creator God.

But we are told little of that time in the Bible record. So the next group of texts concerning the Sabbath promise is found in the Mosaic Law books, especially Exodus and Leviticus. As we have seen in an earlier chapter, the Israelites had nearly forgotten the worship of the one true God. Once away from Egypt, they quickly forgot their awe at God's redemptive power and began to be afraid of life on their own.

In the manna story in Exodus 16, we see how God reminded them that He was their Provider. Interestingly, He chose to remind them of the Sabbath in conjunction with His provision for them. It was as if He were saying, "Remembering the Sabbath means remembering My work. I created you, I rescued you, I will provide for you. You don't have to be afraid. Just rest."

Notice the wording in Exodus 16:29: "See, *the Lord has given* you the sabbath, therefore *He gives* you bread for two days on the sixth day."

(italics supplied.) Also note that this is some time before the writing of the commandments on stone—the Israelites have not yet even reached the wilderness of Sinai. Yet God expects His children to remember His special day and is frustrated when they don't—see verse 28.

We can see His frustration growing throughout Exodus, Leviticus, Numbers, and Deuteronomy. Verse after verse reminds the people of the Sabbath, and some eventually give harsh consequences for ignoring this day. Why? Is God saying, "Do what I tell you, or else!"?

No. If He said that, we'd all be dead. Instead, He keeps using words like "celebrate," "keep," "rest," and His own name—"Sabbath of the Lord." If you have tried to make someone understand the importance of some anniversary to you, and that person has steadfastly made it plain that he/she would rather do anything else on that day than spend it with you, you have some inkling of how God feels about it.

Throughout the years that Israel was a kingdom, and then a double kingdom, Israel and Judah, the people continued to drift from God and His way. His commandments and His promises were less important to them than the rites of the pagans around them. Time after time they fell into political captivity to lands whose religious customs had already taken them captive. Time after time they wailed to God to rescue them—and He did. At last came the great captivity to Babylon, the one where God said, "Don't cry to Me—you will be under captivity for seventy years and not a day less. So pray for the peace of Babylon."

There's an interesting text in 2 Chronicles 36:21: "All the days of [the land's] desolation it kept sabbath until seventy years were complete." At least the land got to have rest at last! Meanwhile, the people had plenty of time to think, and mourn, and repent.

Imagine the depressing task of being a prophet at this time! That was Ezekiel's lot. He had some interesting things to say. Read all of Ezekiel 20. It's a pretty sweeping rebuke, wouldn't you say? Which of the Ten Commandments does He mention specifically? Just two—shunning idolatry and Sabbath keeping. By implication, all of the first four, which are about love for God.

Why? Because they had only broken those? Is it possible that the people had been perfectly loving in their families and among their friends and neighbors, had kept all the other six commandments, but had broken the first four? Not a chance! Once again it is made clear that it is the relationship with the Father that matters—all else follows that. Why, then, is the Sabbath so central? Is it really a must, or is it just a nice idea, when you can find the time?

Through Ezekiel, God tells us plainly. Verse 12 of chapter 20:

> "And also I gave them My sabbaths to be a sign between Me and them, *that they might know that I AM the Lord who sanctifies them."*
>
> Verse 20: "And sanctify My sabbaths; and they shall be a sign between Me and you, *that you may know that I AM the Lord your God."* (Italics supplied.)

To me, these are the quintessential Sabbath texts. They say why. They promise that if I will remember to share God's special day with Him, I will never forget who I am, and Who He is. What a promise! If I could keep that straight in my head, wouldn't it follow that all the other problem areas in my life would come under control, too? These texts also lay to final rest the charge that Sabbath keeping is legalistic. The whole point of the Sabbath is sanctification by grace—resting in His perfect provision. It's impossible to truly keep the Sabbath and still be a legalist. It's also impossible to be a legalist and still keep the Sabbath. One or the other will have to go, once you truly understand the Sabbath rest.

Well, the Israelites thought they'd learned their lesson once and for all. When they came back from captivity, the first thing they did was dig out the books of the Law and relearn them. You can find the story in Ezra and Nehemiah. There's a particularly beautiful one in Nehemiah 8. The people are in tears of grief for their disobedience, and Ezra tells them, "Don't cry. God has forgiven you completely. We have today, and we can start again. The joy of the Lord is your strength, not tears!" And they celebrate wholeheartedly.

How long did it last? By chapter 13 of Nehemiah, that restorer of Jerusalem has to get stern about repeated and unrepentant breaking of the Sabbath by working, and by buying and selling. In verses 17 and 18, he says, more or less, "For heaven's sake, how do you think we got in this mess? Do you want to go into captivity again? I don't!" And he has to make strict rules to ensure their obedience—strict rules that eventually began to backfire.

An Old Testament study of the Sabbath could not be complete without Isaiah 58. Once again, God tries to explain what He meant the Sabbath to be. Although this was written before the above situation occurred, it addresses the kind of attitude that can come from beginning to honor rules too much. If you could put the whole chapter in a few sentences, it might go something like this:

> "You think because you carefully do 'all the right things,' I should listen to you! (verses 1-5). All I want you to do is love, because then I'll be right there with you, (since you can't love without Me), and oh, the blessings I'll bring you! (verses 6-12). Can't you understand the Sabbath isn't your day, it's Mine, and I want to share it with you and make it fabulous and exciting and delightful?" (verses 13, 14).

So we end the Old Testament with two main principles about the Sabbath. First, God made it to be a holy Memorial Day of His creation and dominion. Second, it is the sign that our sanctification comes from Him, and not from anything we do. The few rules that God gives us for the keeping of the Sabbath go hand in hand with these principles. We are to devote the Sabbath day to worship and fellowship with God, building our relationship with Him, so that we never forget His Lordship. We are not to work, buy, or sell on that day, partly because it is a rest day, but mostly because we cannot work for, buy, or sell our salvation, and that is what the day and the rest represent.

Always, God had some faithful ones, but Israel as a whole did not take these principles to heart. The next centuries of Israel's history saw a new kind of wandering from God. This time the intentions were good, at first. The people wanted to be absolutely sure they would never disobey God's commands again. So they started making rules. Dozens of rules. Hundreds of rules. Thousands of rules! God said no idols—we won't even have pictures! God said don't carry burdens to market on Sabbath—we won't carry any burdens on Sabbath. In fact, we won't carry a handkerchief on Sabbath! Well, it's OK if you pin it to your robe on Friday, within reach of your nose . . .

On His special day, can you hear a lonely Father in heaven, sighing as He watches His children carefully pick their way through the rules, and ignore Him?

At long last came the Messiah. Jesus didn't have to remind this generation of Jews to keep the Sabbath. They kept it. Oh, how they kept it. In fact, they weren't impressed with how well Jesus kept that day holy. What they couldn't understand was that Jesus had a different definition of "holy" than they did.

"Holy" meant set aside for God, not set aside for rules. Nothing had changed except the direction of the people's sin. Their fathers had gone off the road to the left—they went off the road to the right. God was still where He had always been: right in the center.

In the Gospels, Jesus shows us how it's done. He worships God on the Sabbath. (Mark 1:21, 6:2; Luke 4:16, 31, 13:10; etc.) He shares time, friendship, love, and His healing presence on the Sabbath. (Mark 3:1-6; Luke 6:1-11, 14:1-6, etc.) He reminds us that the Sabbath is the Lord's day, not the Law's day. (Mark 2:28; Luke 6:5.) Then He ends His ministry on Earth by resting the Sabbath day from His work of re-creation, just as He had rested from His work of Creation.

Finally, some people listened! They saw the face of the Father in His Son, and they fell in love. A wave of change wrapped the globe—a whole "new" message. (Same old one God had always been saying, but when it dawns on *you*, it's new!) The Messiah has come, and you know what He said? He said salvation is not what you do, or even who you are, it's who God is! You can climb into God's lap and relax, just like those little ones did with Jesus! Isn't that great?

In the early church, then, the emphasis is on entering in to the rest of the Sabbath. It wasn't so much that they preached about the Sabbath day—that was taken for granted. It was more that they used the Sabbath to preach the wonderful news that Jesus had died to set us free from the penalties of the broken law. And that He lived to give us the power to keep and treasure it anew, if we only would rest in Him and in His salvation.

Every single text in Acts that mentions Sabbath (there are nine) tells of the new Christians, teaching and preaching this good news to growing crowds. And, of course, to growing opposition. But the rest and peace that Jesus has given them is sufficient even for persecution.

Naturally, there are still legalizers. Paul has to warn against them in Colossians 2:16. And it is to them that the one treatise on the Sabbath in the New Testament is addressed. It's found in Hebrews 4. This letter is written to people who are meticulously keeping Sabbath rules. They know to the minute how long the day is, and what one should or should not do on it. What they don't know is that it is the Lord's day, and it was intended for rest. Read and study this whole chapter, especially if you, too, are tempted to honor the day instead of its Maker. In my New American Standard Bible, the word "rest" is mentioned ten times in the first eleven verses!

What does the writer mean by rest? Shall we sleep all day? No, this rest is a state of mind—it's something we are to "enter into." Enter into where? Look at the last verse: "Let us therefore draw near with confidence to the throne of grace . . ." The implication is that the Sabbath is an entering in to the very throne room of God. If you and I could enter the very control tower of the universe, and see how calm things are there, how unworried God is as He interweaves the paths of all His children and the threads of history, that would be restful indeed! We could stop being so scared, couldn't we?

There is one last passage that deals with the Sabbath, although it is not immediately recognizable, and won't show up in your concordance. In Revelation 14:6, 7 we see an angel flying in "midheaven, having an eternal gospel to preach to those who live on the earth, and to every nation and tribe and tongue and people." (That about covers the population, I'd say.)

And what is this eternal gospel? "Fear God, and give Him glory, because the hour of His judgment has come; and worship Him who made the heaven and the earth and sea and springs of waters." Now, that sounds familiar. That sounds like God's signet ring again. The sign of His dominion and glory, God repeats, as He did in the fourth commandment, is that He is the Creator. The Memorial Day of that Creation, and of Jesus' dying act of re-creation, the day that God promises will help us to remember and follow Him, is the Sabbath. And the two angels who follow this one, in verses 8 to 11, warn that those in the last days who forget or refuse to accept God's rest and salvation are in deadly peril. Don't forget! Remember!

Jesus is still not through creating. He's going to do it again. He will come, and take all those who have stuck by Him through thick and thin, and He's going to make another new world. And then what? Isaiah pictures it for us.

> "For just as the new heavens and the new earth which I make will endure before Me," declares the Lord, "so your offspring and your name will endure. And it shall be from new moon to new moon and from sabbath to sabbath, all mankind will come to bow down before Me," says the Lord (Isaiah 66:22, 23).

The next verse, while figurative, makes it clear that once again, the Sabbath is a Memorial Day—this time a memorial of the death of death, and of sin, forever! Amen! Come, Lord, Jesus! And until You do, come to me every day, and in a special way every Sabbath, and never let me forget who I am, and Who You are.

How?

Ask yourself:

What does the word "Sabbath" mean to me?

Do I really have a Sabbath? Why, or why not?

What is the most special thing about Sabbath to me?

How can I make the Sabbath more meaningful . . .
. . . for myself?

. . . for those around me?

In what ways do I believe work is necessary on Sabbath? (See John 5:1- 18.)

Are there ways I am trying to work for my salvation?

What things might I buy or sell on Sabbath?

Are there ways I try to buy or sell my (or others') salvation?

What human rules have I added to Sabbath keeping? Why?

In order to build my friendship with the Lord of the Sabbath, this week I will:

CHAPTER SIX

Family Matters

When I AM the center of your life,
you shall look upon those two through whom I gave you life
with a reflection of the same love and honor you give Me.
I shall be the foundation of the family,
and the family shall be the foundation of a long and fruitful life,
and of a secure and enduring society.

Paul calls the fifth commandment "the first commandment with promise." That means for our purposes, it's a promise within a promise. "[With God living in you, you will] honor your father and your mother, that your days may be prolonged in the land which the Lord your God gives you."

It seems simple and straightforward. We have a tendency to read a verse like this, say "OK" and go on. But . . . does it really mean you'll live longer if you respect your mother and father? As a parent myself, I could see how that might sometimes be the case! But I have a feeling that's not exactly what God meant. Let's look a little deeper—ask a few questions. Why is it that this particular commandment is linked to a promise, and why this particular promise?

God is about to take the Israelites into the Promised Land. He seems to be saying that if they honor their parents, their life there will be long, and by extension, prosperous. Since we are not Israelites, and have not been given the Promised Land, there must be a special meaning in it for us. It could be heaven, which the term "Promised Land" often signifies. But surely this promise has more immediacy than that. As you'll notice in Bible study, questions usually lead to more questions. What is a promised land? Why is Canaan called that? The answer to that one will take us back to Abraham. And to another question: What exactly did God promise Abraham?

Genesis 12:1-3 is where it all started.

> "Now the Lord said to Abram, 'Go forth from your country, and from your relatives and from your father's house, to the land which I will show you; and I will make you a great nation, and I will bless you, and make your name great; and so you shall be a blessing; and I will bless those who bless you, and the one who curses you I will curse. And in you all the families of the earth shall be blessed.' "

I wonder what Abram would have thought if he had known God was going to fulfill this promise several centuries in the future?

Well, the centuries had passed, and of the million or so people there at Sinai, the vast majority were Abraham's direct descendants. The rest had made a choice, and so received the spirit of adoption, and were now heirs according to the promise. (See Romans 8:17.) Many of this vast crowd were weaned on stories of the Promised Land, but did they remember the rest of the covenant promise? Did they know God's whole purpose was to make of them a great nation, which would be a blessing to the world? Did they remember that this promise contained the seed of The Promise—the Messiah?

And what about us? Are we heirs according to the promise? Do we live in the Promised Land? Are we a light and blessing to all around us? Do we eagerly promote citizenship in this wonderful Land?

You see how many questions Bible study leads to! Some of them aren't always comfortable ones. I hope some answers are also forming in your mind. I hope a vision of the Promised Land and all it can mean is dazzling you.

Suppose the Promised Land, like the kingdom of God that Jesus was always talking about, is more a state of mind than a place. He always talked as if the kingdom of God was right here—right where we are. Or more accurately, right where He is. He seemed to think of it as an un-secret society, spreading everywhere, flavoring everything like salt, bubbling up in unexpected places like yeast, effervescing like wine.

He paid for lifetime memberships for everyone on earth, so it's free—no dues, no fees—all you have to do is confirm your membership, and then keep coming back. Surely this is a Promised Land indeed, one flowing with the milk of God's Word (1 Peter 2:2), and the honey of wisdom (Proverbs 24:13,14)!

But that's only one phrase. That's the "land the Lord your God is giving you." When we look back at our promise within a promise, we find we still have more questions. How does it mean we will prolong our days in the Promised Land? And what in the world does this have to do with honoring your parents?

I think almost everyone would agree that the family is the basic building block of any society. It's almost a truism that when the family begins to break down, society will start to break down, too. Respect for parents leads to respect for other authorities, and a loving, secure home is not a good breeding ground for crime. Therefore it makes sense that God would tell these slaves He's trying to make into a new society to train their children to obey and respect them. Only . . . that's not what He said!

Now, isn't that odd? These are adults. The children are there, too, but surely God is not suddenly speaking only to the children. Could it be that He knows the best way to teach our children to love and honor us is to let them see us loving and honoring our own parents, and for that matter, our husbands and wives?

Marie is a small, timid woman married to a large, not-timid man. They never miss church, and Tom is vociferous in his participation in Bible study and prayer. He is also vociferous on the subject of women and their place. When Tommy Jr. speaks sharply to his mother, Tom growls, "That's your *mother* you're speaking to, young man!" and spanks him. But no one ever actually hears Marie give an opinion of her own, or even finish a sentence. And she still has trouble getting Tommy to obey. I wonder what Tommy is really learning about honoring women, or even his parents.

Harold and Ann have been married for nearly 40 years. He loves his mother very much, and naturally she visits frequently. In the early days of their marriage, when Mother voiced minor criticisms of Ann and her ways, Harold—trying to honor his mother—never said anything. If Ann spoke to him about it in private, Harold said she was overreacting. "They're only minor criticisms, after all. Mother doesn't mean anything by them."

It's true that when Harold is near, Mother seems kind enough. But when she is alone with Ann, she makes it clear that Ann was never good enough for her boy. Little by little over the years, the small arrows have multiplied, and today, Ann is tiring of trying to stem the bleeding. Ann's question: She, too, wants to honor Harold's mother, but at what point does putting others first become self-damaging, and therefore no longer honorable? My question: Is Harold truly honoring either his mother or his wife?

It can be a tricky proposition just figuring out what honoring someone really means, let alone accomplishing it. The matter becomes even more complicated when we realize that, in this un-secret society also known as the Promised Land or the Kingdom of Heaven, we are all one family. We have mothers and fathers and brothers and sisters in the church, too.

When Dorothy or Sue (yes, their real names!) give me loving advice, I listen. They have been walking with God since before I was born. They've raised children, they've been through births, deaths, marriages, and even divorces. Their battle scars mean something to me. So even when they tell me something hard—and occasionally they do—I listen. My children see that.

On the other hand, when I drive home from church grumbling about the pillars of the church—"They think if everything isn't done just their way, the church will fall!"—my children see that too. Our children see truth of the love and honor we demonstrate to our pastors, elders, church workers, and peers. They see. And they imitate, I promise you.

Most of all, they see the love and honor and unquestioning obedience we show to the Father of our family. The fact is, in this society, we're all children. If we let God live in the center of us, He will create in us a humility and contentment that will automatically result in love and respect for others, including our children. And then, God promises, our lives will be long (eternal, in fact) and fruitful in the kingdom of God

Just one more thing about this promise. Did you notice the shift? The first four we studied were all about loving God. And in fact, Jesus said in Matthew 22:37-40 that the first and greatest commandment is to love God with all you have and are, with every fiber of your being. That must come first. We have no chance whatever of obedience, or any of God's promises becoming real in our lives if God does not live in our hearts.

But now we've made the shift from loving God to the second great commandment Jesus cited—loving others as we love ourselves. At first sight, the six commandments dealing with love for humanity begin at home. But in fact, they begin closer than that. Not only is it impossible to love others without letting God live in the center of our lives first, it's impossible to love ourselves, either. Have you noticed that?

When you begin to lose your focus on the great I AM, you begin either to hate yourself directly, treating and speaking of yourself in destructive ways, or to preen yourself, desperately seeking the love—or at least the flattery—of others in the vain hope that you will feel more worthy. On the other hand, when the axis of your world is God, there is a calm certainty of value deep within—impossible to describe to one who has not experienced it, impossible to forget once one has.

Yet, time and time again, we slip off center. Usually when that happens, we try frantically to find that feeling of love again. Look for it from someone else. Try drugs, try TV, try good works. If we could only be more loving . . .

No. If you have trouble with any of the Ten Promises, go back to promise one. Put God back in the middle. He knows how to fix everything else. He knows how to love you. He knows how to give His own love to you to share, how to enable you to love and honor every member of your family, whether they love and honor you or not, and even how to honorably and lovingly keep people from harming you.

He knows how to make your home His home. It's a promise.

How?

Ask yourself:

What does it mean to honor one's parents? Does it mean to do everything they say? Does it have that meaning at one point in life, but not at another? If so, when does it change?

In what ways do I find it easy to honor my parents?

In what ways is it difficult?

What are my favorite things about my mother? My father?

What if my parents and I had a painful, or even an abusive relationship? Then what does this promise mean to me? (See Psalms 27:10, 89:26, 103:13; Isaiah 9:15-16, 66:13; John 20:17, and more)

Who are like fathers and mothers in my church? In what ways can I show honor to them?

For parents:

In what ways do I show love and respect for my children?

How am I teaching them to show respect to me, and to others?

What difference will it make in my life today, if I think of and speak to God as my very own Father?

CHAPTER SEVEN

Abundant Life

When I AM the center of your life,
Your focus shall be on Life.
You shall look at yourself and others
with a deep desire to find and affirm Life,
never to denigrate or destroy it.

Since this is one of the Ten Promises on which Jesus Himself gave a commentary, we would be wise to go there first in our study of it. In Matthew 5:21-26, Jesus explains how the sin of murder, as all other sins, begins in the heart. He says anger and name-calling are as evil as killing someone! This is pretty radical. In fact, if one sees "thou shalt" as "you'd better—or else!" then Jesus has just gone from difficult to impossible.

And in most of His hearers' minds, that's exactly what's happening. They depend on their ability to perform exactly what the law requires to keep them in God's favor. And while many of them may, at one time or another, have been tempted to murder someone, they've managed not to do it. So they believe they've kept the law.

Now here's this young Preacher announcing that if you've ever been mad, or called someone an idiot, you're as guilty as if you had killed! Are you in that crowd? Do you hear—really hear—what He's saying? Have you ever lost your temper? Called someone something? So have I. We're in trouble, aren't we?

Now, wait a minute. Here we are being negative again. Why did Jesus do that? Why didn't He say what He wants us to do, instead of what He doesn't want us to do? Well, He did. He spent the whole rest of that sermon—the whole rest of His life—telling and showing us what it means to spread life, instead of death. He even showed us what kind of anger is godly, as with tears in His voice, He tried again and again to warn His beloved Pharisees, and His bride, Israel, of danger and destruction ahead if they would not listen to Him.

So let's listen. Let's find a few of the places where Jesus demonstrates the divine character as pointed out by the sixth promise. We'll extrapolate from them what He would like us to do to make this promise our own.

We'll start where we ended last time—at home. Let's look right here in Matthew 5, at verses 23 and 24.

> "If therefore you are presenting your offering at the altar, and there remember that your brother has something against you, leave your offering there before the altar, and go your way; first be reconciled to your brother and then come and present your offering."

It's interesting the way this is worded. Jesus doesn't say "if you remember you haven't forgiven your brother," although that is surely important too. He says, if you have offended your brother, and *he* has something against *you*; in other words, you are the one who needs forgiveness in this instance. It seems clear to me that the person in this story, on the way to talk to God, has been reminded by God that there is a sin that needs confessed to a human first. This is not necessarily intended to be an actual blood brother or sister, but in my experience, it's by far the most likely.

I don't mean just as children, either. Sure, my brothers and sisters and I fought like the proverbial cats and dogs when we were young. But, I'm ashamed to admit, I've been reduced to literal, screaming, tearful *fights* with one or another of them in our adulthood! Rarely, thank God, but it's happened. I can't even imagine that happening with any other adult.

Aren't people strange? You hurt most the ones you love the most, just because your lives rub together more. And let's not make any excuses. Sin is sin, and a little death occurs every time. Let's ask forgiveness and thank the Lord on our knees that forgiveness has been, at an unimaginable expense, made available!

Next let's look at the stories of Jesus blessing the children. These stories are found in Matthew 19:13-15, Mark 10:13-16, and Luke 18:15-17. In order to understand how we can be like Jesus in this regard, and what it has to do with the sixth promise, it would be worthwhile to find out what it means to "bless." My Greek lexicon says the word used here means "to speak well of, to thank or invoke a benediction upon, prosper, or praise."

There are also two other components of blessing mentioned in these passages: laying hands on the children, and praying for them. When I read this I wonder: doesn't that mean that when we speak poorly of, complain to, or scold, to neglect to pray for, or to pray in a negative spirit, neglect to touch, or touch in negative and painful ways, we curse our children? Awful thought, isn't it?

After the above definition, do I need to tell you that my children, whom I love more than anyone else on the planet, have experienced all of these at times? How grateful I am that Jesus promises, if I let Him live in the center of my life, He'll bless my children, (yours, too) through me!

Moving out of the immediate family and into the family of God, let's look at the way Jesus brought life to those society cast out. Take a look at the story of the good Samaritan, in Luke 10:33-37. Compare the actions of the robbers, the priest, the Levite, the Samaritan, and the innkeeper. Which brought death, and which brought life? The way we usually interpret the sixth commandment, the only ones who broke it in this story are the bandits. Do you think that's true?

Then there is the adulterous woman in John 8:1-11. This woman was guilty. She had been caught in the act. Set aside the fact that the man had not been brought to justice. Set aside the fact that it may even have been a set-up. She was guilty. And she stood in the presence of One who knew no sin. Her sin demanded a curse, not a blessing, and Jesus knew it.

> "See, I am setting before you today a blessing and a curse: the blessing, if you listen to the commandments of the Lord your God, which I am commanding you today; and the curse, if you do not listen to the commandments of the Lord your God, but turn aside from the way which I am command-ing you today" (Deuteronomy 11:26-28).

But Jesus also knew something no one else there knew. He knew He had come to her world precisely for the purpose of paying her debt of death, and bringing her life. So He blessed her instead. Understand—He did not set her free with a stern warning. That command, like all of His biddings, was an enabling. It was a promise.

God shows this same attitude in many other places in the Bible. Jeremiah is one of the best places to look. Jeremiah is called the weeping prophet with good reason. His books are filled with tears and warnings, with dreary lists of the incredible evil perpetrated in the name of the Lord. God pulled no punches when describing either their sin or what would happen to them because of it.

That's not the surprising part. The surprising part is how, in the middle of the curses are blessing after blessing after blessing. Like this one:

> "Thus says the Lord God of Israel, 'Like these good figs, so I will regard as good the captives of Judah whom I have sent out of this place into the land of the Chaldeans. For

I will set My eyes on them for good, and I will bring them again to this land; and I will build them up and not overthrow them, and I will plant them and not pluck them up. And I will give them a heart to know Me, for I am the Lord; and they will be My people, and I will be their God, for they will return to Me with their whole heart" (Jeremiah 24:4-7).

There are dozens of those in Jeremiah, maybe scores of them, and more in Isaiah. That's the way God talks to confirmed sinners. "Come back! Please come back! I will heal you!"

In light of this attitude on God's part, how are we to respond to those who know we know they are openly sinning?

"Brethren, even if a man is caught in any trespass, you who are spiritual, restore such a one in a spirit of gentleness; looking to yourselves, lest you too be tempted. Bear one another's burdens, and thus fulfill the law of Christ" (Galatians 6:1, 2).

"Walk in a manner worthy of the calling with which you have been called, with all humility and gentleness, with patience, showing forbearance to one another in love, being diligent to preserve the unity of the Spirit in the bond of peace" (Ephesians 4:1-3).

"Make my joy complete by being of the same mind, maintaining the same love, united in spirit, intent on one purpose. Do nothing from selfishness or empty conceit, but with humility of mind let each of you regard one another as more important than himself; do not merely look out for your own personal interests, but also for the interests of others" (Philippians 2:2-4).

Let me tell you about my mother. She's one of those women who seems to be everybody's mother. No, don't go thinking in terms of stereotypes. She's far more likely to ride bikes with you (and skin her knee doing it) than to bake you cookies after school. She never keeps you from playing in the rain or getting dirty, or tells you to put on a sweater because she's cold. She used to be able to climb a tree faster than any kid in our neighborhood. She probably still could, only her heart is acting up these days. It's slowed her down some, but so far as anybody can tell, hasn't actually prevented her from doing anything she really wants to.

What I mean when I say that she's everybody's mother is that you can tell her anything—anything in the world, and she'll listen, and try to understand, and *she'll love you.* She won't condemn, even if you know perfectly well she doesn't approve of or believe in what you're doing. She won't try to change you. She figures that's God's job, and she wouldn't know where to start, anyway. She knows He still has a lot to do in her, so why should she look down on any other struggling sinner?

In her varied career, my mother has listened to, loved, and prayed with and for babies, children (millions of 'em!), teenage runaways (her own and others'), gang members, Vietnam vets, silent stroke victims whose only words are in their eyes, the very aged, the very disabled, stressed-out mothers, lonely people, overwhelmed people, depressed people, sick people, rich and poor, beggars and thieves, butchers and bakers and at least one Indian chief! She has been unloaded on by complete strangers. How does she do that?

Where do we get all that life, that we can afford to throw it around on each other with such dazzling abandon? Here's where: "The thief comes only to steal, and kill, and destroy; I came that they might have life, and might have it abundantly" (John 10:10).

Will it ever run out?

"And this is *eternal* life, that they may know Thee, the only true God, and Jesus Christ whom Thou has sent" (John 17:3, italics supplied).

60

"And he showed me a river of the water of life, clear as crystal, coming from the throne of God and of the Lamb, in the middle of its street. And on either side of the river was the tree of life, bearing twelve kinds of fruit, yielding its fruit every month; and the leaves of the tree were for the healing of the nations. And *there shall no longer be any curse*; and the throne of God and of the Lamb shall be in it, and His bond-servants shall serve Him; and they shall see His face, and His name shall be on their foreheads" (Revelation 22:1-4, italics supplied).

How?

Using a concordance or a list of Jesus' healings, make a list of how many times He used touch to accomplish His miracles. Why do you think this was so?

Look through Jeremiah and Isaiah, especially after Isaiah 40, and find as many blessings as you can. Were there conditions to receiving these blessings? If so, what were they?

Brainstorm about places in Scripture where God is shown or named as Lifegiver. Look up some of them and ask Him to show you how to reflect this characteristic of His in your keeping of the sixth commandment.

Ask yourself:

What are some of the ways God has blessed and affirmed my life?

What are some ways others have blessed and affirmed my life? Have I thanked them?

How often, and in what ways do I bless the members of my family?

the members of my extended family?

the members of my church family?

strangers I may meet?

Ask God to show you how to bless those with whom you come in contact today.

CHAPTER EIGHT

Marriage Made in Heaven

When I AM the center of your life,
you shall center your marriage on Me also.
You shall love that one and only beloved
with the love which I shall give you —
love which shall bear all things, believe all things,
hope all things, and endure all things,
love which shall never fail.

What is adultery? Sex with someone who's married, but not to you, right? Or is it sex with anyone you're not married to? Or is it a lot more than that? This is another subject Jesus elaborated on. In fact, He saw fit to talk about marriage and divorce quite a lot, and it is found in every single Gospel. You'll find His commentaries in Matthew 5:27-32; 19:3-12; Mark 10:2-12, Luke 16:18; and John 8:3-19.

In Matthew 5, Jesus adds to the above definition by saying that if one looks with lust on another, adultery has already been committed. So it starts long before sex. You don't even have to be married. None of the Ten Promises is for only one class of people, and this one is not only for married people. Clearly Jesus has a broader definition of adultery than we usually do.

And here's something a little unnerving. Close study will show that in several of these passages, Jesus also says a man can "cause" a woman to commit adultery by divorcing her when she is not guilty of impurity herself! This cannot mean one person's action makes another impure, since God has already made it clear in Ezekiel 18 and elsewhere that one is only responsible for one's own sins. So what does it mean? Does Jesus' definition of adultery include ramifications that are not even sexual at all?

In the dictionary, the word adultery is at the end of a whole list of "adulterate" and "adulterous" and so on. They all come from a Latin root which means to falsify, surprisingly enough. It also means to add a "prohibited or inferior substance" to something, making it "inferior, impure, not genuine, less valuable!"

Would it be stretching too far to suggest that in God's eyes, anything less than 100% pure love (which comes only from God) is adulterous? Can we adulterate love by adding a little "prohibited substance" like selfishness, or make it less genuine with a little falsity? Because if so, then we can indeed make a person feel inferior, not genuine, and definitely less valuable. That would tangle with the sixth commandment, too, wouldn't it?

Several times, Jesus reiterates His (that is, the Creator's) view of married love. "The two shall be one flesh"—one of the very first promises in the Bible. And once again, in the light of yet another overwhelming enlargement of a command, we could, like the disciples, get discouraged and exclaim, "It is better not to marry!" Except, we're looking at these commands in a new way. And there's still John 8.

You'll recognize this story from our last chapter. It's the one about the adulterous woman who is caught in the act and brought to Jesus. Did you notice that verse 12 tells how to do verse 11? My Bible even has a "therefore" at the beginning of verse 12. This time, read all the way to verse 19. There it is—the promise.

Walk in Jesus, have the light of life, you'll know Him and His Father, and They won't judge by the flesh.

She was guilty. But now her guilt was gone. Praise God!

What a world of difference this seventh promise could make to our marriages! I wonder, is it just chance that it's the seventh—the number of perfection? Or could it be that the perfect marriage God sees when He looks at two of His children who are holding each other and looking back at Him is a reflection of His unity in three Selves. Could He see a reflection of His unity with His bride, the church, and in some ways, a culmination of all the six promises that have gone before?

How do we start learning about perfect love, so that we can flood our marriages with it? Well, you could start at Genesis and go to Revelation, and then you could go back again. Our study of love will take our whole earthly life, and then spill over into eternity, and never end there, either.

Have you ever noticed that the Bible begins and ends with marriages, has one whole book on the subject, and Jesus started His ministry at one? He must think they're pretty special. In the interest of space and time, let's pick one bit to study. It's hard to choose, but let's go to the obvious place—1 Corinthians 13, and let's see if we can learn something all new and not obvious at all.

1 Corinthians 13 has three main sections. The first section, verses 1-3, lists some of the spiritual gifts Paul has been speaking of in the last chapter, and shows that they are all useless and powerless without the one great fruit of the Spirit—love. The second section, verses 4-7, describes this spiritual love in glowing terms. The last section, verses 8-13, speaks of ever growing maturity, culminating in the perfect maturity of eternal life with the God of love Himself. Let's look at these three sections with marriage in mind, and ask God what He wants to teach us.

Look at verse 1. Have you ever tried "eloquence" on your husband when he was already upset with you? In my experience, neither the tongues of wives nor of angels will succeed in dragging his mind around to see things my way. My multitude of words is like nothing so much as a clanging cymbal to his weary ears. But when I've calmed down and recognized those telling words "my way," then I suddenly realize love may have had little say in the whole discussion. Even if I'm right (verse 2), love matters more to my marriage than deep insights and knowledge, or even than faith. Faith without love, that is, which sounds like presumption to me.

Now verse 3. Have you ever played the martyr in your marriage? Have you worked hard and given all your possessions to feed the children, and delivered your hot, weary body to take care of the house, and the yard, and the cars, and then discovered with dismay that your wife still asks if you love her?

Well then, what is love? Now for the gleaming heart of the chapter, shining like a diamond surrounded by velvet. If—and this is a very big if indeed—if we understand that commands are promises, then the power to love comes from God! This is a very discouraging chapter if you think it's holding up something you are supposed to DO. But if you understand that God is saying to you, "This is how I AM, and if You let Me have My way with you, this is how you SHALL BE, I promise," then it's exciting instead.

Just think—you shall be patient, even unto the seventy times seventh time you have to pick up after her. You shall be kind, even if he just said something unkind to you. You shall not be jealous, because you shall be completely secure in God's love for you, and in His control of the things that scare you about this lifelong commitment thing.

You shall not brag or be arrogant, because you'll be too busy telling your friends how wonderful that beloved other is. Your actions shall show Who is at your center, and you won't feel the need to seek your own way, your own rights, your own wishes. You'll know they're being cared for. Instead of becoming provoked and upset at wrongs, you'll forgive and actually forget! You shall not rejoice in man- or woman-bashing, or in the world's ridiculous or wicked portrayals of love and marriage; instead, you'll be a living example of heavenly marriage.

You shall bear it when she's cross, believe him when he says he's sorry, hope for a coming day of perfection for both of you, and endure anything you have to—together—until then!

Best of all—can you believe this?—your love will never fail! Because it's God's love, and He never fails, and He promised His love would grow in you, where His Spirit lives! Is that incredible, or what?

I can almost hear you giving a big sigh of happiness and then look-ing around at your world, sighing a different sigh altogether, and saying, "Well, that's all very well, but it doesn't look like that at my house!" Good thing Paul put on that third section.

Here Paul explains that the things of this world, even the great and good things given by God for our edification, like prophecy and tongues and knowledge, will end someday. Right now, we know only in part. After 20 or 30 or 60 years of marriage, we still surprise, even shock, each other. We even prophesy in part. In other words, the people who speak for God because He gave them a message to pass on for Him only say that message the best they can, and there are still imperfections in it.

We see faint images of God in our marriages and in our mirrors, because we do the best we can to follow Him, like a little child walking in Daddy's footsteps. Sometimes we cry because we make such a mess of it. But God promises that if we keep our hands in His, and keep stretching our legs beside Him, someday we will know Him and each other as fully as He knows us. Wow!

Notice the first two words of verse 13. "But now . . ." Now while we are waiting for that day, faith and hope and love are alive in us. We don't have to wait for them. They're here, because the Spirit is already here, having been given as our guarantee.

That's enough for me.

How?

Here are twelve adjectives applied to love in 1 Corinthians 13: 4-7. Meditating on each, ask God to show you a specific way to make it a reality in your life and relationships.

1. Patient
2. Kind
3. Secure (not jealous)
4. Humble
5. Becoming (in action)
6. Unselfish

7. Forgiving
8. Rejoicing in truth
9. Bearing all
10. Believing all
11. Hoping all
12. Enduring all

If you are single, ask yourself:

How does the seventh promise apply to me?

If you are single and not happy about it, read Isaiah 54, and all the promises you can find that speak of God knowing and providing for your needs. Tell Him how you feel, and write down how you hear Him answering you.

What if you are the only one in your marriage who cares about looking to God? Then how does this promise apply to you?

Ask yourself:
How can I love with unadulterated love someone who does not love me, or loves me with adulterated love?

Take comfort in the knowledge that you are in good company. God's first bride, Israel, was unfaithful to Him over and over. For that matter, so is His second. He still loves both perfectly, and He can empower you to do the same. Be aware that if your spouse or your marriage is harming you, you may have to take the course God eventually took. He never stopped loving Israel, and He loves her still today, but He did end the marriage. I strongly recommend the book *As For Me and My House*, by Walter Wangerin. It is the only marriage counseling book of the many I have read, which shows how to follow, with incredible love, the example Jesus outlines in Matthew 18.

CHAPTER NINE

A Giving Heart

When I AM the center of your life,
I shall supply all your needs.
You shall be so rich in love and well-being
that your greatest joy shall be giving to others,
never taking or harming what they have or are.

There's stealing, and then there's stealing. Grand theft auto. International jewel theft. Shoplifting. Embezzlement. Midnight requisitioning. Forgetting to put the quarter in the cup for soda at work. Tax fraud. Habitually showing up late for work, or doing your own work there, while taking their paycheck. Borrowing without asking. Not returning what you borrowed. Stealing someone's reputation with a whisper or two. Refusing to give back God's tithe of what He gives you. Flirting with somebody else's significant other. Wasting time. Burying talents. The majority of us would never consider ourselves thieves, and probably don't usually think we have trouble obeying this commandment. Until we start really thinking about it.

Obviously, in this eighth promise, God is giving His word that He can empower us not to do any or all of that stuff. But as always, His dreams are much bigger than ours. When I started thinking about this, asking myself what God wants us to do instead of steal (asking myself how in the world I was going to fill a whole chapter with "thou shalt not steal"), I was stumped. Be content with what we have? Well, of course, but what else? Finally it dawned on me. The opposite of stealing isn't not stealing. It's giving.

Take a look back at that first paragraph. See what the opposite of each would be, in this light. Let's see—giving away a car? Or giving a ride to someone who needs one. Giving jewels, maybe to a good cause. Using some of your own supplies at work, paid for out of your own pocket. (Wouldn't that drive the bookkeepers crazy?) Treating harried cashiers as kindly and cheerfully as if they were the customers, and you were the one who wanted them to come back again. Putting an extra quarter in the cup . . . You think of some more ideas. Isn't this fun?

But even giving can go haywire. We can give the wrong things, to the wrong people, for the wrong reasons. And end up in disaster. In fact, I would even say disaster is inevitable, unless we understand the one essential First Fact about giving. We must burn it into our brains and never forget it for a minute, or we will never be givers ourselves. Never. Here it is—have your highlighter ready—God gave first.

GOD GAVE FIRST.

Not only would we have nothing to give if He hadn't given first, we wouldn't even exist if He hadn't given us life. And we wouldn't have continued to exist if He hadn't given everything He had just to give us new life. Jesus' brother, James, put it well. "Every good thing bestowed and every perfect gift is from above, coming down from the Father of lights, with whom there is no variation, or shifting shadow" (James 1:17). He even gave us the freedom to choose evil. Which we promptly did. Then He gave us grace and forgiveness and a key so we could come back home.

Remember it. God gave first. And last, for that matter.

That means there is a First Step to giving, too, if we want it to be real giving. Before you give anything to anyone for any reason, give yourself to God. All of you. (You'll find out later that it wasn't really all of you, even though you meant it to be, and you'll have to do it again . . . and again . . . But that's OK, because He knew that, and He took all 100% of you the first time, and considered it treasure unimaginable.)

As soon as you give yourself to God, you'll find that He immediately starts giving more than ever to you. You'll find yourself overwhelmed, and wish you could give something to Him too. That's when you'll have the first of many conversations that will go something like this:

"I love You so much, Lord. I want to give You something."

"What do you have?"

You look around. All you can see are the things He's given you. Is it OK to give back something He gave you?

Your Father smiles gently. "What is that in your hand?" (Watch out—that's what He asked Moses, remember!)

"My business. You want my little business? It's not even supporting my family yet."

"Give Me your business, and you and I will go far together."

So you do, and together you start using your business, which you thought you had started for profit, to give to everybody else in reach. It's so much fun (sometimes more excitement than you bargained for . . .) that you find yourself offering Him your money, and your health, and your time, and the piano talent you enjoy so much, and it never ends.

Once in a while, you stop and look back and you realize that all you've been doing after all is turning over to Him more little pieces of yourself. The same ones you thought you had already given Him the first time, or at least the thirty-seventh time, and anyway it's all stuff He gave you first. You might feel dismayed and think you've never given Him anything at all. If that happens, just look into His face. You'll see that He seems to think you've given Him the moon. Only, He made that too.

One day, you'll be reading the story of the sheep and the goats, in Matthew 25:31-46. It's an awesome story. In your mind you can picture it—Jesus sitting on His glorious throne, surrounded by all the angels, and dividing up the nations. He divides them all into two groups, which for this story He calls sheep and goats.

[To digress for a moment: If you've ever raised sheep and goats, as I do, you'll know why Jesus uses these terms. My angora goat, Gabriel, is named for his "angel hair," not his saintly behavior! Sheep, in case you *don't* have any, and have wondered, are the ones who are stupid enough to do anything you tell them, including jump off a cliff. Goats are the ones who are smart enough to want to do things their own way. Think about it.]

"Come, you who are blessed of My Father," says Jesus, beaming with excitement, "inherit the kingdom prepared for you from the foundation of the world. For I needed and you gave."

The sheep look bewildered. (Sheep do that a lot.) "But when, Lord? I tried and tried to give something to You, but I never could find anything You hadn't already given me!"

"Believe Me," replies Jesus, "when you gave to My little brothers and sisters, you were giving to Me."

And all of a sudden you figure it out. The thing you're giving to God that He treasures so much (besides yourself—His favorite present) is the joy of giving to His other children, especially the ones who won't let Him give directly to them yet. You see, Jesus doesn't have physical hands and feet of His own in this world anymore. He only got to do that for a little while. Now He has to depend on ours.

When Frank lost his beloved wife of almost fifty years, there wasn't much anyone could say or do. After decades in emergency services, Frank had recognized death coming. He stayed strong for Lois. But he cried in the arms of his friends. They had no answers for him, but they had arms and tears. That was giving to Jesus.

When Frank himself lay dying a few years later, his friends were there again. This time their tears were for themselves. Frank was smiling. He knew he would open his eyes and see Lois. And Jesus would hug his little brother Himself. Until then, Jesus' hands were caring tenderly for Frank in the hands of his family and friends.

I know a person who gives strung-out boys hugs and encouragement, never lectures. *That's giving to Jesus.*

I know a group of teenagers who spend part of their spare time raking leaves or painting for those who can't do their own, and collecting food for hungry families. *That's giving to Jesus.*

I know people who spend week after week, year after year in the children's departments of their churches, caring for God's giggly, wiggly babies. *That's giving to Jesus.*

I know a care center for the aged where the people are truly loved, patiently cared for, and allowed the quirks they've earned with eighty or ninety years of hard living. I know Jesus is there, because I recognize His smile when I see it.

There's a lot of stealing going on out there. That thief of hearts, the prince of darkness, is stealing souls and sanity and sunshine. Jesus needs you and me desperately to help Him rescue, rebuild, and restore what has been lost.

In Isaiah 58, He promises that if we loose the bonds of wickedness, let the oppressed go free, share our food with the hungry, our homes with the homeless, and our clothes with those who need them, and if we do all of this from an attitude that these people are "our own flesh," that we will find in these things our own recovery, and more blessings than we can comprehend. "The Lord will continually guide you," He says, "and you will be called the repairer of the breach, the restorer of the streets in which to dwell."

Like any other dumb sheep, I admit I'm scared. But I want to give Him something. And after all, He did give me these ten fingers, this mind, and this computer . . .

How?

Read Matthew 25:31-46 and Isaiah 58:6-12. List the specific methods of giving named in each passage. Mark the ones that appeal most to you, and ask God to show you how He would like to give these things with you and through you.

Now copy the long list of promised blessings in these passages on 3 x 5 cards and post them somewhere you'll see them often.

Ask God:

What exciting ways can You and I use these resources for others today?

Time:

Money:

Health:

Home:

Work:

Special talents_____:

CHAPTER TEN

A Door Named Truth

When I AM the center of your life,
I shall become for you the Way of Truth,
the Life of Truth.
I shall lead you into all Truth.

It has occurred to me that this list, whether you call it commandments, promises, or whatever, is a ladder. These last few really get down to business, don't they?

Of all the things from which we sinful humans have alienated ourselves, Truth must be nearly the greatest. Truth. What in the world is it? Pilate had a good question. The only truthful answer we can give is, we have no idea. All we can think of is not telling lies, and even then, we probably tell more with our eyebrows alone than we have any idea of. What would it be like to live a life of perfect truth? Think about it for just a few minutes. "Transparent as sunlight," one nineteenth century writer said. Sorry. Not possible. I have too many smudgy places on me.

Some have pointed out that after asking that question, Pilate left, not giving Jesus time to answer. I don't think He would have answered, anyway, because He already had. He had been answering that question for thirty-three and a half years. He came to this planet to answer that one vital question.

I AM.

Jesus had many other names for Himself, besides Truth. He called Himself the Way, and the Life. He called Himself the Door, and the Faithful and True Witness. In this ninth promise, Jesus is saying that He can open the door (Himself) to a new way of life (Himself) in which you and I—believe it or not—can become faithful and true witnesses. Is that awesome? Shadowed and cracked as we are, and let's face it—He never promised to fix the shadows and cracks until He comes again—we can become, in Him, faithful and true witnesses. He will shine out through the cracks, and make even the shadows help to form a picture in our lives of what He is really like.

So, in practical, down-to-earth terms, what does that mean? Let's take a look at what the Bible has to say about truth.

A little study of my lexicon reveals that the word most often translated "truth" (or "faithfulness") in the Old Testament is a contraction of a word which means, among other things, "to build up or support, to foster as a parent or nurse, to render or be firm or faithful, trustworthy, steadfast, established, etc." Isn't that interesting? That means truth is a foundation, a rock-solid one. That's another of Jesus' names, of course.

A common biblical expression is to "walk before God in truth." (For examples, See 1 Kings 3:6, Isaiah 38:3.) In 1 Kings 2:4, God Himself defines this as "be[ing] careful of their way, to walk before Me in truth with all their heart and with all their soul." So this life of truth requires all of myself—an integrated whole—which is where we get the word "integrity."

As we might expect, the Psalms mention the word "truth" more than any other Old Testament book, and also explain it in more detail. Psalm 15 is a mini textbook on the subject. This "citizen of Zion" described by David speaks and lives truth by word and deed. Even in the privacy of his own heart, he speaks truth, and makes vows to himself which do not change with expediency or circumstances. I can't always say that—can you?

In fact, this is one of those Bible passages that can be very discouraging to one who doesn't know—or has forgotten—that all God's commands are also promises. David, in the course of a long and checkered career, certainly learned that lesson, and he knew other hearts like his could use reminding just where that truth comes from. And reminding again and again and again . . .

"Lead me in thy truth and teach me" (Psalm 25:5).

"All the paths of the Lord are lovingkindness and truth" (25:10).

"Into Thy hand I commit my spirit; Thou hast ransomed me, O Lord, God of truth." (31:5). Jesus, at the supreme universal Moment of Truth, found comfort in this one.

"O send out Thy light and Thy truth, let them lead me; let them bring me to Thy holy hill" (43:3).

And on and on. Dozens of times that vital little phrase "Thy truth" appears.

Psalm 119 is clearer yet. It shows that God's law is the truth, (verses 42-45, 142, 151) and that to follow is a choice (verse 30).

The prophets continue the threefold theme:

1. God's Word is the only place truth is to be found.

2. Those who choose to follow Him in that truth are blessed now and forevermore.

3. When truth is forsaken, calamity follows. (See Isaiah 59:4-15, Jeremiah 7:28, Daniel 8:12, Hosea 4:1, and many others.)

In the New Testament, the writer who uses the word "truth" the most often is John—the beloved one, the one who clung the closest to Jesus. His first mention of it, in John 1:14, sums up the teaching of the whole New Testament: "And the Word became flesh, and dwelt among us, and we beheld His glory, glory as of the only begotten from the Father, full of grace and truth."

Come to think of it, that sums up the teaching of the whole Bible! There's the Word that makes things Be, which is therefore by definition Truth. There's the Father and the Son, and the Love and the Sacrifice, there's God—with us!—there's the Grace and the Glory and the Power. There's enough to sing about for millennia on end!

And there, too is the first clear clue of the how. Up to now, while it has been very clear that truth is greatly to be desired, that it comes only from God, and that you must follow God closely to get it, it still hasn't really been clear how it happens. Jesus knew that. That's why He came.

There, in John 1:14, is the beholding or seeing. The rest of John's book is full of that concept. In John 3:21, "He who practices the truth comes to the light." (Where things can be seen.) In John 4:23, 24: "Worship the Father in spirit and truth." (In Chapter 3 of this book, we learned that to worship God was to *see* and adore Him for Who He really is.) In John 14:6: "I am the way, and the truth, and the life," and in 14:9: "He who has *seen* Me has *seen* the Father."

Jesus had already promised in John 8:32 (please notice the wording) "*You shall* know the truth, and the truth *shall* set you free." [Italics supplied.] He now went on to explain that His Spirit, "the Spirit of truth," (16:13) would make it possible for His followers to continue to behold Jesus, even though He would no longer be with them in the flesh.

So in 2 Corinthians 3:18, Paul could say, "But we all, with unveiled face beholding as in a mirror the glory of the Lord, are being transformed into the same image from glory to glory, just as from the Lord, the Spirit."

In Jesus' beautiful prayer in John 17, just so there could be no misunderstanding, He said, "Sanctify them in the truth; Thy word is truth"(v. 17). In one sentence, He had reiterated the lesson of His Old Testament prophets: God is the only place truth may be found, and it is that—His truth (faithfulness)—which sanctifies us.

In Revelation, the Faithful and True Witness commends the

churches for their faithfulness and warns those who are not walking in truth. The issue of all the end-time prophecies is "Who's telling the truth?" And last of all, at almost the tail end of the Bible, is a warning list of those who will not be in the city with God (David's "holy hill"). Is it a surprise that among the list of murderers and sorcerers and adulterers is "everyone who loves and practices lying"?

We have obviously only scratched the surface of what the Bible has to teach on the subject of truth. The more we study the more we'll see that this life of truth, faithfulness, and integrity is the very essence of sanctification. And we know that's a lifelong process. Once you choose to follow Jesus, to walk in His grace and truth, some things will become instantly clearer. Other things will require more study and prayer. Sometimes it even seems that different people get different answers to the same questions.

This is where it gets very sticky. Surely if Truth is absolute it is the same in all times, in all places, and for all people. God, who calls Himself Truth, is "the same yesterday, today, and forever." Right?

So—your friend comes in to work one day wearing a dress that makes her look like a pillow with a string tied around the middle—a pillow in a particularly dreadful shade of green. And with a bright smile, she says, "I got this on sale! What do you think?" Do you say what you think? Why or why not? On what basis do you decide what to say and how to say it? What if it's your boss?

And worse yet, do you or don't you tell the Nazis you have a Jewish family under the floorboards? I've heard it hotly debated both ways. Some insist that God will not bless anything but the factual truth, and that if one tells the truth, God will work it out.

A few years ago I heard a missionary tell of trying to cross a border with a truckload of Bibles where they were illegal. The border guards asked him, "What's in the boxes?"

Naturally, this was just the question he had hoped not to be asked. He didn't believe in lying or covering up the truth in any way. So, with a hasty prayer and a pounding heart, he said, "Bibles."

The guards laughed. "Oh, sure! What's really in the boxes?"

When the missionary insisted they were Bibles, they just let him go, still laughing.

There is no doubt at all that God was at work here. But other Christians believe there is a time when God's people are allowed—even obligated—to mislead others, especially to save lives. Here's an example of the well-known Brother Andrew's point of view. This story is taken from his book, *The Ethics of Smuggling.**

"I am determined not to tell a lie, but I pray mighty hard that I won't have to tell the truth, either. That may sound like an impossible contradiction, so let me explain.

"I said earlier that Godless men who have given themselves over to the service of the devil and his forces do not any longer have a right to the truth. After all, their allegiance is to the one whom Jesus called a liar and the father of lies. As a matter of fact they are not even interested in the truth—and probably don't recognize it when it stares them in the face.

"Now there are several ways that I come at this matter of the truth in dealing with the enemy. Remember, we who love the Lord are in the service of the truth, and know that it is the basis on which God works his miracles. So I want to stress again what I have said before: I do not lie.

"For one thing, I believe in the *concealment* of the truth. Here's an illustration of how that works.

"One Sunday morning, a Christian boy was going to one of the secret house meetings of believers behind the Iron Curtain. Everyone knew that the police were trying to find out where the church was meeting, so his father warned him that day to be very careful to watch out for the police.

"All alone, the boy made his way quietly toward the meeting house. Christians had to go one at a time. Other members of the family would have to go at different times and take different approaches to the meeting place. I have practiced this myself in going to such meetings in Communist countries.

"Walking along happily, he suddenly was stopped by police

who had been hiding behind a tree.

" 'Stop!' they ordered. 'Where are you going?'

"The boy stood there for a moment, determined not to tell a lie, but probably equally determined not to tell the truth. He must have shot a telegram prayer to heaven (which the Lord answers providing you take proper time for prayer when you have the time!)

"He looked the policeman in the eye and with a very sad face (sad because he had been caught!) he lowered his voice for a reply:

" 'Sir, I am going to see my brothers and sisters. This morning we are going to open the testament of my oldest brother.'

"The policeman took pity on him and said, 'All right, sonny, on you go!'

"This boy had really saved the situation for the church. He had not told a lie, but had told the truth in *concealment*, inasmuch as he was dealing with an enemy who was not entitled to know the truth."

Brother Andrew goes on to say Jesus used this same method, quoting Jesus as saying He told the truth in parables so that those who listened for the wrong reason could not understand (see Mark 4:10-12). He also goes on to advocate partial truths, and creative interpretations of the truth. And he gives very compelling reasons, too, showing that some of God's soldiers are called to be secret agents, and pointing out that we all owe higher allegiance to God than to earthly governments.

I can't argue. But I was raised to believe that telling the truth in such a way as to mislead is still lying, and that there is *never* a justification for lying. Whether I still believe that, I am not sure.

It gets worse. There are actual biblical incidents which seem to condone—no, to *advocate*—outright lying. One is in Joshua 2. When the Israelites finally came to the Promised Land, a Canaanite woman named Rahab hid two of the spies Joshua sent, and told the authorities straight out that she didn't know where they were, and "They went that way! If you hurry, you can catch them!"

The next chapter of the story, in Joshua 6:17, 22-25, shows Rahab and her family saved, which seems to imply that her actions were at least condoned. And Hebrews 11 includes Rahab and her welcoming of the spies in the same list as Abraham, Isaac, and Jacob, not to mention Moses and the rest of the Hall of Faith. Was she blessed because she lied, or did God bless her anyway, because He knew she didn't know better?

And what about that very confusing story in John 7:8-10? Jesus said He wasn't going to the feast, but then He went secretly! Read it for yourself. Did Jesus Himself lie, or at least twist the truth? Or is there more to the story that we just don't know?

Unfortunately, discussions tend to get bogged down and angry right about here. I've seen whole Bible study classes divided over some of these texts. And I certainly don't propose to give the quintessential answer! But here's something to think about. Is it possible that truth could be absolute and immutable not in a rigid, static way, like a rock, but in an organic way, like a living, loving God?

No, no, hold the stones, I don't mean truth is situational. But I do mean it's up to each person to ask God what to do in a given situation, and not to judge what He told someone else. One thing is certain: it is possible for us to be so caught up in digging out the cold, hard facts of a case that we forget the people—the ones Jesus risked eternal death for—and thereby miss the Truth altogether.

At the end of His Word, right after that grim list of who doesn't make it, Jesus, being Jesus, ends with a promise. "Yes, I am coming quickly . . . . The grace of the Lord Jesus be with all. Amen." His grace and truth are with me! Yes!

Brother Andrew, *The Ethics of Smuggling*, (Wheaton, Ill.: Tyndale House, 1974) 112-114.

How?

You may wish to take your own Bible(s) and concordance and do a deeper study on truth than we have done here. If so, be sure to ask the Holy Spirit to guide your study and show you the personal truths He has for you.

We learned three principles of living a life of truth.

1. Truth comes from God alone, and is expressed in His law.

2. We have a choice whether to walk in His truth or not.

3. If we choose to walk in His truth, we do so by beholding Jesus continually.

Ask God:

How can I see Your truth more clearly;
in Your law?
in all of Your Word?

Are there areas in which I have not made the choice to follow You, or have taken back my choice? I give You these areas now:—————

————————————————————————————————

How can I behold Your face today . . .
in nature,
in the Word,
in others,
in my own heart?

CHAPTER ELEVEN

Abiding Contentment

When, at last, I AM all of your life,
you shall abide fully in Me, and I in you.
Your life shall overflow
with such deep and lasting contentment
with all that you have and are
that you shall not even desire anything that is your neighbor's.

I have a confession to make. I have always thought this was sort of a tacked-on commandment. I wondered why a little thing like coveting got a place with murder and adultery. Now that I'm studying the commandments as a ladder of promises, I have a whole different viewpoint. This seems to me to be the pinnacle. The final, tie-it-up-with-a-bow promise of the one thing everyone wants more than anything else—absolute peace.

Isn't it reasonable to say that those who covet are doing so because they don't have peace, and they think some other thing, or condition, or something will give it to them? She has $20,000 more per year than I do, and she seems content. Sure he's happy—he has a beautiful wife who adores him!

Doing a word study on the word "peace" in the Bible would be a pretty daunting task. There are three and three-quarters columns in Strong's Concordance on peace, and you know how tiny that print is! But if you start scanning those seemingly endless columns, they soon begin to sort themselves into some simple categories. From Genesis to Job, almost without exception, peace is used either in expressions and greetings such as "hold your peace" and "Peace be to you," or in the term "peace offerings." It's amazing. I never saw so many peace offerings in my life. It made me wonder, what exactly is a peace offering? It must be something important.

At first glance, a peace offering would seem to be either an attempt to make peace with God, or to show that you have peace with God. And if you accept the truth that all the offerings of the ceremonial system were meant to point forward to Jesus, then it immediately becomes clear. All those offerings culminated in the one Sacrifice in which, as Paul says in 2 Corinthians 5:19, "God was in Christ reconciling the world to Himself, not counting their trespasses against them."

In other words, God was the one who made peace with us. That means human peace offerings have to be a response. And guess what? The lexicon says that particular word means an obligatory offering of thanks. Interesting. The Israelites were thanking God for something that hadn't even happened yet, in the stream of time. But God considered it as having been completed "from the foundation of the world" (Revelation 13:8, KJV).

So peace with this warring planet, and with my warring heart, began with God long before I was born. And of course, peace continues to come only from God.

From Psalms to Revelation, the majority of verses mentioning peace are promises. Dozens of them—maybe hundreds of them! Just reading the phrases in the concordance alone is enough to make your heart swell. And if you look up the whole promises, you discover gems like these:

"The Lord will bless His people with peace" (Psalm 29:11).

"The steadfast of mind Thou wilt keep in perfect peace, because he trusts in Thee" (Isaiah 26:3).

And just a few verses later—look at this diamond! "Lord, Thou wilt establish peace for us, since *Thou hast also performed for us all our works*" (verse 12, italics supplied. Shall I supply a few exclamation points, too?).

"For you will go out with joy, and be led forth with peace; the mountains and the hills will break forth into shouts of joy before you, and all the trees of the field will clap their hands" (Isaiah 55:12). One of my favorites, this one has pulled me through many difficult situations.

Isaiah is so full of promises of peace that it's hard to pick only a few. How about these two? " 'Peace, peace to him who is far and to him who is near,' says the Lord, 'and I will heal him' " (57:19). "For thus says the Lord, 'Behold, I extend peace to her like a river' " (66:12).

Unfortunately, Jeremiah is mostly full of warnings of no peace, and rebukes to those who promise it falsely. Yet here is God, speaking right in the middle of all this turmoil: "For I know the thoughts that I think toward you, saith the Lord, thoughts of peace, and not of evil, to give you an expected end" (29:11, KJV).

And at the end of your turmoil: "Behold, on the mountains the feet of him who brings good news, who announces peace!" (Nahum 1:15).

We could do this all day, and we haven't even touched the New Testament. But I still have questions. What exactly is peace? It's easy enough in church to listen to that story about the artist who portrayed perfect peace by painting a picture of a bird in its nest at the tip of a branch hanging out over a wild, rushing waterfall, and nod your head and say, "Amen!" It's even sometimes easy, there in your pew, to leave those troubles that plague you outside the church door, at least for awhile, and believe that maybe God knows what He's doing, after all. "It's like an ocean," you agree with your friends in the foyer. "There might be all kinds of waves on top, but down underneath, all is calm."

Then you walk out the church door, and like a flock of vultures, there are your pains and heartaches, hovering over your car, waiting to escort you home. Your mind goes to the Williams family, who sit together in church every week, while you sit alone, knowing you'll go home to the same old indifference, or even ridicule. You remember the health glowing in the faces of the youth and wonder, with a tremor, why the doctor wants to see you so urgently. Or maybe you can't even get to church, but sit in a wheelchair and watch the world pass you by. Could these thoughts turn covetous?

Peace! Is it really there, under the stormy ocean? Is it possible to feel it, without drowning yourself, and your normal human emotions, to find it?

I have another confession to make. This has been a serious issue for me for some years now. When God says, "I will supply all your needs," (Philippians 4:19) what does He mean? He doesn't always mean you'll have food to eat, or enough warm clothes, or even that you'll keep your life. When Jesus says, "Let not your heart be troubled, nor let it be fearful" (John 14:27), does He mean it's wrong to feel fear?

I have to tell you, I'm not comfortable sharing this. It would be one thing if I could say, in a sort of saintly way, "I used to wonder about this, but then I understood. Let me tell you how it is . . ." Only I can't. I don't understand.

I've read and studied Job three times through, because it's about this very topic. Job and his friends go around and around the question of unreasonable suffering and human emotion, just as I have, and you know what the answer at the end of the book is? God comes to Job, and He says, "There is no answer, at least not one I'm going to share with you. You are never in your earthly life going to understand. All you have to figure out is this: are you going to let Me be God, or not?"

Which takes us right back to the beginning of these Ten Promises. And my answer is the one Jesus' disciples gave when He asked, maybe plaintively, "Are you going to leave Me, too, as all these others have, because they couldn't understand Me?" Peter and I say, with a mixture of determination and perplexity, "But, Lord, where else would we turn?" (John 6:67, 68, slightly paraphrased).

I don't know why the children you raised so carefully and lovingly are taking drugs. I don't know why your lovely Christian wife left you for another man, and thinks it's God's will for her life. I don't know why you have only months to live, or why your mother doesn't know who you are anymore. I don't know why my brother suffered such pain his entire life that death at 36 was a blessing. But I do know there's no one else to turn to but God. Like Jacob, I may wrestle with Him, but I'm certainly not going to let Him go! And thank God, He's not going to let me go, either!

That said, I can at least share with you a few things I've started to figure out.

1. It's OK to ask God questions, even to wrestle with Him, as long as you never let go.

2. It's OK not to have the answers. I can't tell you how much I dislike this one. But you know what? God has all the answers. Honest. And He really doesn't need my help to run things.

3. It's OK to have feelings. You can throw yourself in God's arms and yell when you're angry. He has broad shoulders. You can cry to Him when you're scared, you can even pout to Him, though He's likely to snap you out of it in a hurry. Just as I'm writing, something has occurred to me. Maybe that's what peace is—not being free of fear and anger and so forth, but knowing Jesus is right there to take care of you when you're feeling them.

4. Recently a new insight came to me while I was thinking about John 14:27. Jesus said, "Peace I leave with you; My peace I give to you; not as the world gives, do I give to you." I've always taken that to mean that the world gives peace that doesn't last, and isn't real, while Jesus gives the real thing, and it lasts. And I still believe that. But I wonder if He also meant that His peace was so different that it would not be recognizable as peace by the world's standards.

The world defines peace as tranquility, contentment, lack of conflict. Jesus seems to define it as laughing in Satan's face while he cuts you down with his machine gun, just because you've read the end of the book, and know how the war will end. And after all, if I had to choose between tranquility here and tranquility in heaven . . .!

5. This I do know, and this I will stake my life on, and stand on to

the day of my death. If peace doesn't mean anything else at all, it means eternal salvation, starting now, and the eternal presence of my Lord, here, with me, now. The more trials we have, the more we will be able to say with all our hearts:

"Our God whom we serve is able to deliver us . . . and He will deliver us . . . but even if He does not, let it be known . . . that we are not going to serve your gods" (Daniel 3:17, 18, italics supplied). (And that includes gods of fear and anger and worry and doubt.)

"Though the fig tree should not blossom, and there be no fruit on the vines, though the yield of the olive should fail, and the fields produce no food, though the flock should be cut off from the fold, and there be no cattle in the stalls, *yet I will exult in the God of my salvation.* The Lord God is my strength, and He has made my feet like hinds' feet, and makes me walk on my high places" (Habakkuk 3:17-19, italics supplied).

"For I am convinced that neither death, nor life, nor angels, nor principalities, nor things present, nor things to come, nor powers, nor height, nor depth, nor any other created thing, shall be able to separate us from the love of God, which is in Christ Jesus our Lord" (Romans 8:38).

And how have we been convinced of these things? We believed them with our heads when we heard them preached and sung. But we know them with our hearts because we learned them by bitter experience. And someday we'll be grateful. Yes, grateful.

In the meantime, we'll walk with Jesus, and we'll treasure His peace in our hearts, and coveting others' pacifiers won't even occur to us. Instead, we'll give away God's peace every chance we have, because peacemakers are the most blessed of all. They're the children of God! (Matthew 5:9.)

I'll end with a beautiful blessing, and my favorite peace promise of all.

> "The Lord bless you, and keep you; the Lord make His face shine on you, and be gracious to you; the Lord lift up His countenance on you, and give you peace" (Numbers 6:24–26).

> "And God's peace [shall be yours, that tranquil state of a soul assured of its salvation through Christ, and so fearing nothing from God and being content with its earthly lot of whatever sort that is, that peace] which transcends all understanding shall garrison and mount guard over your hearts and minds in Christ Jesus" (Philippians 4:7, Amplified).
> Amen!

How?

Ask yourself:

Do I covet? If so, what? (Don't answer too quickly. You can covet not only things, but feelings, situations, even the way someone else's children or spouse behave!)

Now ask God:

> In each of these things I covet, what is the true blessing
> I really crave, that's turned inside out in my envious wishing?

Think of a time in your life when you really saw and felt God's peace, even in the midst of a painful or difficult situation. Try to describe your different feelings as well as you can.

Now think of times or issues in your life in which you have diffi-

culty accepting God's peace. Dig deep and ask yourself honestly:
What is it that I really fear?

How can I make the decision to accept God's working
and have His peace about this?

One more thing that I have learned the hard way is that peace will percolate into my heart almost like magic, the minute I begin to sing praise songs. I have sung them with tears streaming down my face while rushing through the night to a hospital, while on my way to divorce court, and beside more than one grave. Why not post a list of your favorite hymns and praise songs in a conspicuous place, and practice "counting it all joy," even the trials? (See James 1:2-4.)

CHAPTER TWELVE

The First and Last Word

Let's take a look back, and summarize what we've learned.

We've realized that, given the language of the commandments and our knowledge of the character of God as He has chosen to reveal it, we can look at His commandments as promises. We can see God saying, "This is how I am, and if you let Me, I will make you like Myself." With this exciting concept in mind, we have looked at each of the Ten Commandments in a new light.

1. God wants to live at the very center of our lives. We already live and move and have our being in Him. He wants us to be aware of it, and of Him—all the time.

2. He promises that He will be Alpha and Omega to us, if we worship Him by seeing Him as He really is and praising Him, serve Him with passion and excitement, love Him, love Him, love Him, and treasure His commandment/promises. He even promises to carry those blessings on through the generations.

3. He promises to give us His own name, with all the rights and privileges pertaining thereunto.

4. He has given us a whole special day every week, to spend with Him, to renew our hearts, minds, and spirits, and to remember that He is Creator and Re-creator. On that day we worship Him and rest in Him,

thanking Him for the finished work of our salvation, and we don't work, buy, or sell, showing that we cannot work for, buy, or sell salvation.

5. He promises to renew our family relationships, enriching our ability to love and honor our parents as part of loving and honoring Him. Even if our parents do not know how to love us, from a safe place in God's arms, He will enable us by faith to love them as He does.

6. He promises us new life, and new eyes to see and affirm life in those around us, so that our words and deeds are never killing or destructive, but always building up.

7. He promises to teach us to love purely, never adulterating love with selfishness, falsity, or any other sin. He also promises to miraculously turn our marriages into something dazzling, like His own relationship with His church.

8. He promises to richly supply all our needs, and to make us generous givers, not miserable graspers.

9. He promises to be Truth to us, and to fill our lives with all Truth, so that all the world will see Him in us, and falsehood will be anathema to us.

10. To crown all, He promises us such peace that it is not even understandable to the human mind, peace that will only glow more brightly the more conflict the enemy hurls our way, peace that we will want to share with others, never wishing we had what they have.

Amazing, isn't it? It's like a whole new Decalogue, like something we've never heard of before!

Or is it?

When Jesus was asked what was the greatest commandment, He quoted something written around 1500 years earlier—Deuteronomy 6:5:

> " 'You shall love the Lord your God with all your heart, and with all your soul, and with all your mind.' " Then He added, "This is the greatest and foremost commandment. And a second is like it, 'You shall love your neighbor as yourself.' On these two commandments depend the whole Law and the Prophets" (Matthew 22:37-40).

Then Paul said, "Love does no wrong to a neighbor; love therefore is the fulfillment of the law" (Romans 13:10).

Then John said, "God *is* love" (1 John 4:8, italics supplied).

A nineteenth century writer named Ellen White called the law "the transcript of God's character."

And centuries and centuries ago, God already promised, "I will put My law within them and on their heart I will write it; and I will be their God, and they shall be My people" (Jeremiah 31:33).

The inescapable conclusion is that when God is finished writing the law—the transcript of His own character—on our hearts, it will become the transcript of our characters! If that isn't shocking, I don't know what is.

But it's nothing new. It's clearly the teaching of the whole Bible. And to me, one of the main proofs that the Bible really is the Living Word of God is the fact that no matter how many times you read it, the Holy Spirit will lead you to learn and understand things you never realized before.

As I finished writing these pages—in fact, after I thought the book was finished—I realized something new. It concerns the ark of the covenant. In fact, it concerns that very name. Would you believe it never dawned on me that "ark" is just an old-fashioned way to say "box" or "container"—that the famous, revered ark was simply a fancy box in which to keep the covenant?

And what was that covenant? The Ten Commandments. See Exodus 25:16-22; Deuteronomy 10:1-5; I Kings 8:9; and II Chronicles 5:10. And what is a covenant? A set of promises, of course. This particular covenant was signed by the hand of the Father, sealed by the blood of His Son, and delivered by the Holy Spirit. Rather than being peripheral or intimidating, the law of God is the center of the whole Bible. It and the Gospel are one and the same, because Jesus is the Word of God's covenant, spoken for all to read and understand.

So the box we keep the covenant in today is called the Bible. It's the whole reason for the Book. And the "earthen vessel" into which God has promised to transfer the covenant—if I really want

Him to—is me! (see 2 Corinthians 4:5-7.)

"Now abide faith, hope, love, these three; but the greatest of these is love" (1 Corinthians 13:13).

May the Father, Son, and Holy Spirit shine His love on us, and in us, and through us, now and forever.

If you enjoyed this book, you'll enjoy these as well:

The Scripture That Changed My Life
Ron and *Dorothy Watts*. Forty true stories of men and women who found strength through a single passage of Scripture during times of personal crisis. The testimonies of John Bunyan, Joni Earickson Tada, Corrie Ten Boom, and others are included.
0-8163-1583-3. Paperback. US$10.99, Cdn$16.49.

Powerful Passages
Ron and *Dorothy Watts*. Stories of well-known historical figures and contemporary individuals whose lives were changed from a single passage of Scripture.
0-8163-1337-7. Paperback. US$10.99, Cdn$16.49
.

In the Light of God's Love
Ty Gibson. With simplicity and pathos, this book addresses our personal and corporate need to rethink our distinctive doctrines and realign our Christian experience in the radiant, healing light of God's love.
0-8163-1334-2. Paperback. US$9.99, Cdn$14.99.

Order from your ABC by calling **1-800-765-6955**, or get online and shop our virtual store at **www.adventistbookcenter.com**.
Read a chapter from your favorite book
Order online
Sign up for e-mail notices on new products